A Vision of Oneness:
Adjusting The Notions of Separate and Alone And Recognizing The Unrecognizable

by, Drew A. Stevens

Thank Your Guide, LLC © 2011

A Vision of Oneness:
Adjusting The Notions of Separate and Alone And Recognizing The Unrecognizable

ISBN-13: 978-0-9836875-1-1
ISBN-10: 098368751X

Published by:

Thank Your Guide, LLC
USA

First Printing, May 2011

Publisher's Cataloging in Publication
(Prepared by Quality Books Inc.)

PS3619.T4788U55 2011   811'.6

QB110-700456

Contact info: www.thankyourguide.com

Thank Your Guide, LLC
P.O.Box 1841
Wheat Ridge, Co. 80034-1841

Dedicated to:

The Source, The Light, The Spirit Guide, and D.N.A.

...And, I would like to thank: my philosophy professor in college... my parents, relatives, friends... the many musical vessels... the many truly enlightened authors... the founders of America... and the many unsung heroes worldwide, who keep things as good as they are.

Acknowledgements:

Authors: Sri Chinmoy, James Redfield, Alan Watts, Scott Mandelker PhD, W.Y. Evans-Wentz, Ernest Holmes, Henry David Thoreau, Native American Folklore, Mythological History Books, and the many Meditation Guides.

Special shout-outs: The Physics Of Space And Time, Animals, Plants, The Dictionary, Art, Health, Smiles, Vehicles, Computers, Stereos, Beds, Silence, Indoor Plumbing and Electricity, Friends, Compassion, Empathy, Love, and The American Democracy!

...And a extra special thanks to you, the reader... For giving...
...An ear to hear, the time of day, and a mind to triangulate this challenge.

Contents:

Part One Detailed:

About the author...

I'm a 20 year seeker of the many forms of enlightenment ...And a studious practitioner to the service to others philosophy... kind of, a search for higher truths, for others.... I was told a couple bits of guidance early on..."Always be true to yourself"...."Always keep an open mind"... and, "If you cant live up to your word, your nothing". These three wise ones are the most powerful and shaping bits of advice I ever got... they have guided me through all decisions, and how I programmed my subconscious...and at 18, I was given a Buddhist book on meditation.... and it took me in with its sensitivity to the most simple, yet existential perspectives of reality.... and the ultimate challenge... to attain enlightenment.... well, I just had to try.

I struggled with the idea at first, as I had no real reason for wanting enlightenment... Man had existed fine with out it, in many parts... yet ignorance is a problem...so many would never try to attain it... I was mostly on my own... a personal decision....I had finally deduced that it was a duty I owed existence.....creation...to find some truth, to the essence of all I believed to be true ....and to try to find the The Truth.

My first experience, after four years of preparing, was a sitting meditation that took 21 days straight... little eating.... rarely sleep....just sitting.... infect, controlling breathing to the point of what seemed like indefinitely long breaths.... It was becoming a new experience... the fluctuation of time became recognizable...seeing moments shift from one to the next...I was meeting and reaching a profound transcendental meditation experience... through years of preparing, and a lot of writing, reading, thinking, talking, and meditating.... and I was finally doing a real meditation... the going with-in potential was finally conceivable.... and on the 17th day I received a vision.... of a purple and green angel fish... sitting right in front of my awareness... eyes closed... in perfect real time clarity... like video, but no water... just the fish, and its brilliant colors and motion in the fins...It was amazing .. I'd heard of visions before, and this was so profound...I opened my eyes, for no reason but ecstaticness... closed em' again, and got kind of sad to just see blackness... but soon after, the visions started to flow again...and what a flow at that... turns out the dreaming part of the brain... that makes those reality scenes in dreams, can do that when your awake... I don't know how..... I just watch.... But I give credit to the light of mind, mother nature, and the source of consciousness....I worked hard preparing for enlightenment for years and through positive expectation...I manifested a higher truth for myself....simply by belief, faith, and dedication.

This grew into learning about the polarization of orientation, or rather, how kind a soul is... the mean ones, and the ones of love... they don't fight each other...They try to out smart one another in their consulting our souls... As the guidance goes, if one is ever overwhelmed, or under pressure from negative vibes... just say no way!.. Don't try to get the upper hand...just ignore negativity... and they'll get drown out with the recognition of all the love that's always around.... and pending recognition...our spirit guides sit back, never parenting, never defending ... just sitting silent, till we realizes the difference between positive spiritual energy and negative...and only give positive. ... harder than one would think, due to the one pointedness and limited perspective ability of mind in the finite form....trapped in time and squeezed, such that one cant even see there's a choice, or remember any of the love.... eventually it becomes, the individual and the guide walking through time...

I took a path less taken...one that can find a way to go within to the inner recesses of the soul and bring that information back....It's a gift from my higher self... unity of consciousness exists...I don't have it, yet... but I have glimpsed a thing or two...and have a lot to share as a result.... for when one finds certain truths with empirical evidence, but can't prove it to anyone... all they can do is be honest and straight up... no room for spin, lies, or ego building... my lack of strive for self made me a good potential mouthpiece to this grand vision.... as I really just want to share an idea of us, with a higher energy, ...and a vision of unity with the divine within, and throughout the universe.

Through an openness to sharing, staying true to the most high truths, and working for the light of love...I guess I deduced a philosophical ring on existence ...for myself.... but its been no easy ride....but in fact, a really hard challenge....I learned to see multiple perspectives, and can find balance to all sides.... is where I shine best.... I had to go through many tests of integrity to get where I am...staying true to my stated philosophy...and is my main accomplishment, ...and the enlightenment attainment clues held with in these texts, are somewhat, to very practical...as much ,comes from personal experience.... and also from very kind, and intelligent sources...The books I have sought are in the hundreds...All holding powerfully revealing pieces to the puzzle of life.... and the mysteries of the unknown...which aren't that unknowable, once the dots are connected.

This is the accumulation of over twenty years of dedicated study in many aspects of the metaphysical... and the revealing of the wisdoms, of the metaphoric wordage, of a reality of light and wonder…all leading to a final realization of the presence of god, …and that we have been consulted by spirit guides, or older souls all along…just unrecognizably so… but the message gets through, none the less…and we can see the hallmarks of the two sides, good and negative, clear as day, if we check it in the right light…and in reality.. They're the angel on one shoulder, and the devil on the other … to everyone … always… and 95% of us mostly listen to the good ones… 5% the bad… and of the 95%, only 33% listen to the good guides exclusively… the rest get mixed messages… due to not being able to recognize the archetypes of the service to self…. and harboring many of them… who are masterful liars …. they seek to confuse, worry, invalidate, cause anger, depression, and fear… The good ones seek to remind us of all we have to be grateful for…all we have to look forward to at the next level…. that all fear is erroneous… faith in self… faith in nature… and faith in god is simple and very satisfying, and doesn't require a religious affiliation, though it does help the realization processes…. and that all frustration, and anger can be avoided by finding the reasons… once understood why… anger is ridiculous…Empathy and understanding should be the mature stance.

So… I eventually realized… I am working with a spirit guide… to get to a certain goal…communion with the unity of the universe…. and graduation to the ancient angelic community… and to do as much service to others stuff … while I'm here… which led to this…

… In continuum…I look up to Gandhi, Jesus, Siddhartha, Mother Theresa, The Dali Lama, and any other saint of service to love for divinity….I've been to many different churches to learn, observe, and reflect …for a theological pursuit…my favorites are small nondenominational Christian, small humble Buddhist, or self church …Where I try to meditate, for spiritual purposes…I listen to the most enlightened music, nonstop…. I have become an solid circle of truth representation of my field of study…yet always learning, decoding, and piecing together anew…And due to the rarity of my study … Enlightenment truth seeking, and god realization…I have found something anew… something many, have not seen before… It is my contribution to the mystery,…I am just a dedicated seeker of the transcendental essence of existence, and a truth preservation to reverence for it… And to finding new perspectives.

In this work, I purport a belief in a source divine within, which is the unity throughout the universe, and loves us beyond belief…That we are of pure light consciousness awareness…and that we are not far from other souls, of past and present, via the unity of consciousness…And that some of those souls are very, very old...And that they interact with us like guardian angels, as spirit guides, as intelligence consultants... To find the truth, the way to the next level, and the key to the balance of life...or, playin' fair and showin' care!

So,...if one wants to believe in a continuance after death.... then what goes on after we die, very well could be a splitting into three ways... one that joins old souls who are bullies, if so inclined...one that joins old kind souls, if like-minded...and one that goes back...and does it again, like this life...till one learns the lesson of how and why to do onto others, as one would wish back for themselves....Thus we find a challenge, a duality, and an opposition to our quest to find some truth...termed "the downward pull" by the ancients...is giving a fearless confront to souls who choose the negative...selfish, without any care for their actions repercussions, or for any others affected ....these poor saps, "angry/jealous gods" or "negative nellies", are an opposite intention to wise spiritual decision making...and easy to spot!

So with the logical acceptance of a continuance... an old, wise guide...An old, and impotent, and unwise, counter guide....Who can be ignored once spotted...And then comes the light of the source....A recognition that takes practice...but once held....Can bring a sense, that all that happens in life, is the mere tip of an iceberg, of what's going on behind the scenes .

This word enlightenment can seem foreign, but if one ponders it enough... they see it's probably occurring all the time...everywhere...to everyone... in subtle, to blatant forms...but it is truth, love, and understanding that occurs to all eventually...Even if not till death...it is wiser to count on it.

As the saying goes....Ya never know what ya might have missed, had ya not tried.....True with love affairs, jobs, and promotions....and with enlightenment....Simply knowing your working for a good cause, and helping people, is the mantra of the enlightened ones...as they know...life is time...and time is ceasing... and ceasing means, there is no more....yet, we continue!...A renewal of a now...every few micro seconds....a perpetual ceasing and renewing...simultaneously, always.

What this may be telling us is that this plane of existence is temporary, only...but something of it all is of a permanent nature... ...And it lies within.

...This is my most recent account of attempting to realize god, as a presence.... Conceptual transcendental idealism.

Intro

There is a lot to life, death, and the in-between that is not so easily noticed. We are mostly on a fast track of patterns, with scarcely a thought of something unseen...or a potential for new discovery, pending. And on occasion, in a moment of silence or clarity... we can sense we're a part of something more... something bigger than life.. Something beyond life... Something invisible... Just beyond the surface level of awareness... is our essence.... and a whole lot more. I wish to convey the insights I have found.

There are certain words... like... the light, transcendentalism, the source of life, a spirit guide, one universal love, unity within... that hold certain potentials for realization... And, there are writings of old... like the Tibetan text, the Dead Sea scrolls ... among many...that hold certain potentials for realization... Along with the many modern writers of the most enlightened recognition levels, who have made open, the potential that always was...for anyone who has the mighty achievement of recognizing the formless light within.

They all offer glimpses, views, and visions of a reality just beyond the one we know well, and take for granted, so easily. These pieces to the big puzzle are very linkable, and after too long, anyone can start to see the picture the puzzle reveals, when complete, is a new outlook on life, dying, and real existence to come.

I have been working on a theory that we can walk into new discovery, through realization....we've all heard the meta concepts...God, Angels, The Light...But to try to find em'...To maybe finally find something we had never, and would never have seen, had we not tried to plow through, mull it over, piece it together, and go within.

This is a new approach to writing a book, and to conveying intelligence insights...It comes in the form of snippets... and one liner quotes, poems, and inspirational randomness... Written in triple dot... to convey the concepts, more than speak in conversational perfection... Designed to be easily grasped ....so one doesn't get boggled down with sentences piling up... just simple, and sometimes humorous, conveyances' of the highest perspectives, and the deepest insights I could muster.

There is a lot of slang, mistakes, made up words...please, let it slide... it's like that for reasons... I'm not just skipping editing and proper grammar because of laziness. There is a feel one gets, seeing it as it was originally made...That shows the unfiltered freedom of writing spontaneously! ...And the innocent nature of my writing....As I hope not to offend anybody, or to try to incite a debate like stance...Just a free flow of the "out there" god talk I like to juggle.

The first part is a series of inspirational notes I started sending to my friend one day...because he was down in the dumps...and I wanted to cheer him up. So the night before I'd prepare some "off the wall" inspiration.... it went on for a few weeks, and became a personal realization aid to my beliefs... and a process of bringing them all together, for easy, consolidated recognition, therein.

The second half is reflections, cognitions, ideas, realizations, insights, that have hit me time to time, or heard through one of my many intelligence sources...music, church, or reading... over the six months that followed...where I'll go to write it on some piece of paper... hence the one-liner nature of it.

So, when reading, try to keep perspective, that I'm simply talking inside lingo to an old buddy...in letters from me to him...the observer in this series gets to see a snap shot of my beliefs, talked with someone, who shares the same...It was never intended to be read as my personal statements to the world...though it can seem that.... Rather, I hope to share these, only to help bring the reminders and inspiration they brought to me... and to show something I would have never written into a book to publish, had it not been written under the intimacy of to a friend, first...

If I could make one request to the reader...let it flow as rhetorical humor, wacky god talk, an attempt to make believe, a dream, a poem, just a bit or two of inspirational reminders.... Only meant as esoteric potentials....Not a debate of reality truth... Please take the ones that don't work for you, with a grain of salt, or just discard them. ... to many,... none of these recognitions will seem valid....to others... they will help put all of the pieces together...It helped me a lot... and I wanted, so much, to share it with someone else...

...Hope it helps!

The Recognition Challenge:

1.....In-light!

It's all or nothing with finite mind vs. Infinite access... Enlighten-ment from the soul mind can occur when one truly get the mean-ing of the empty mind... For when you really get it... See it face to face... Pure emptiness...The Truth....The Lie... The conspiracy within... And realize that's all you really are... And all your hopes and dreams are held in an idea... Within a mere concept of self-hood.... And in this perspective, of actually seeing through the pettiness and delusion of ego,... you can drop it... Recognize the source of consciousness is sourcing...from with in you...through you...as a now, and you are already at one with the light of pure consciousness... Drop all notions of past self, for a new self... enlightened, realized... always flowing with the source ...in recog-nition of it!;)

2.....Time

The out side world is in time ... It is ever ceasing.... by definition it is finite...but time is also going on in the inside, too... it is unclear as to weather it is flowing in or out of us... but the books I have, say it flows out, from with-in first...that the flashlight of awareness we shine around...gives existence to whatever we direct aware-ness at...The rest of the time things are only ideas... Crystalized thought on a holographic blueprint.... and time really doesn't exist either... because it really cant be measured... it travels too fast to gauge.... Time is the grand wizardry of existence, here... It is so limiting... so constricting... yet smooth, and subtle... But also rigid, and demanding... it is a curious creature indeed... The cool thing is that's of source divinity... and it is graceful beyond belief.

So....
An Infinity is within.... conspiring...yet recognizably so... Seeing past the illusion of a finite mind is with in our ability.

And going within, is a feat...that's up to us... and is within our capacity as well.

013

If we spend all time in pattern mode, chasing stuff in the outside world... We solidify a finite reality... And thus live in a finite mind.... Never believing we were meant to move and grow in the infinity within...We cut ourselves off from new discoveries within our mind, brain, subconscious, and soul... 4 fantastic infinite fields of exploration... Waiting… pending recognition of.... On everyone... All the time....

Enlightenment does exist! For, It is real existence itself, waiting for us to drop the illusory, distorted aspects, of the primitive level recognition, of reality's depth.... And prepare to meet the ancient.... DNA(molecular level awareness), the clear light of reality, the angelic antiquity, the collective unconscious of earth's past.... And good old god, The Source.

As soon as one truly let's go of the notion that the objective world exists... So will the finite mind, cease to exist.

3.....The Light

Realizing the light is a subtle process.... First, one must see that sight is light, minds eye and physical eye...what you think is being shed light upon.... by you and from you.... It remains clear and neutral, for it is up to us to realize it's love... And it's sacredness. Second is adjusting self concept to being viewed from The Light... Self-consciousness becomes uncomfortably squeezed...and you can deduce what a trillion year old intelligence might think of your twenty ought years of accumulate.
Remember love gets tough.
Third we need to realize the light source being the same in every living being.... The unity kind of axes out self.... There is no existential battle of wills... One has to surrender to the flow of consciousness... The light is a natural ego dropping mechanism ... As it destroys delusions of selfhood... In it's unity.

It knows all... Has total awareness.... Is disbursed universally, on all planes.

Knows your current status in reality's pecking order of most care is most high.... Knows your lessons, and emphasizes them. Cares more than you'll ever imagine, and cares less, as self is twofold.... Half being eternal, and the other mortal.

It never ends... The quest for the light.... The seeking of illumination.... The illuminating of the seekers...

The light is the grand mystical everythingness everywhere at once... it is able to reveal and clue us to itself ... if you can listen like a lover...

We will see everything for how it really is once we've removed our notion of separate.. Which is to see the light, and is to flush our self-imposing limitations from our minds... By our own realization!:)

4.....Collective Unconscious

There is a movement towards enlightened en mass... It's as if the collective unconscious of earth is being squeezed so to be more in awareness of each other and our thoughts. I wondered if it was just me, but I've triangulated off others, and I see it's everyone. Most seem unrecognizing, but I sense, they can sense it at the subconscious level....A new vibe of things showing up here or there.
It's like god can turn the light switch on for everyone at once:)... Keep it off', is what she'd say.... she's busy enough.. But it's a neat vision....
I think it is calling out for pioneering... Something is more at our minds fingertips than ever before... The collective of ourselves, shared...unity with the separately conceived;)

5.....Higher Self

The higher self, or the super-subconscious, or the soul is so illusive in conceptual terms, yet it is always in place and on point as much as it can. It seems to conspire with old souls, DNA and the source. It knows em', and knows we don't, but were not supposed

015

to, until were ready, we seek sincerely, and polarize and spark ... meaning to become polarized towards showing love for others or not... and to show a lot of energy put into ones chosen direction.... Then it seems to take form in effect... Until the quest and questioning of the where's and why's ... Souls seem to be naturally, virtually nonexistent, and inescapably undecided and self focused.... So each life holds a potential to awaken, and grow polarized...And even with knowledge of the higher self... Doesn't ignite one... Ahhhh, the lesson... Instills a balanced sense of earning the attainment/accomplishment.

It's hard to recognize, hard to realize, hard to remember, hard to hold truth preservation to, hard to work with others who are not sparking... But it helps if one keeps questing, though no one else ever seems to.

Illuminated is the goal... Tis where the 3 minds are most closely aligned and can thus transmit information throughout with minimal distortion from the poor subconscious(it's conditioned by liars.... Of the 3rd & 4th kind)...in 3rd from everything we've learned that wasn't true, and in the 4th is the spirit liar of old, and well, he's had plenty of time to whisper lies...
Point being... Souls know guides face to face.. Lying ones too, but it can't tell the difference most the time.... Aka...their undecided new souls, just like us.... Pending polarization realization just like us.... To embrace the lessons, the service to others philosophy brings to us all!
Souls operate independently to us.... Are free to move about... Plotting endlessly.... Very alert... very aware...in recognition of all memory's, and thus should be cognizant of the permanency of them....
Must even get frustrated with its lower self...us?
Hummm.... What does it think of all this? Probably no worries.... Maybe its diluted to think there's nothing that really matters...or very worried...about graduation? or wanting to play selfish games with other immature souls? ... In the end were all gods and goddesses, in theory... One can't imagine what a million lifetimes will do to a permanent memory mechanism.

Keep in mind, service to self leaning souls do occur ... And their human containers are none the wiser...all souls have to hide and they know this, it's like some rule they are aware of, and don't break.

Thus function to meditation... Brainwave necessary for updating.

6.....Going Beyond

Going beyond/ breaking through to another level of conscious being-ness is possible, but belief that one can is most important!

There are many examples we have... One is spontaneity.... Like in music...Ad-libbing.... Shootin' from the hip...it is faith one can do it, and does! Confidence... Fake it till ya make it.... Puttin' on a front... But still prone to doubt...
One must also imagine and visualize it happening.... the movement.... The change... The limitless potential access ,..The becoming one with the light...
Imagining the unimaginable.... Like recognizing the unrecognizable ... It is possible:)
The power of imagination becomes a vehicle for change/ metamorphosis...
If love, selfless pursuits and the unity vision are the premise ... It will grow and bloom in a good way...most make it bloom with ego building as the major premise...forgetting its the main point to all this in the first place...dropping the lie,
finding the truth.

Working with higher powers like DNA, The spirit guide, and the source are illusive, never showing blatant signs, always subtle... They are so much more aware of us, than we are of us ...always.... And we're always falling into attitude traps... Always stemming from a self based distortions.... Hence dis-believing in the presence of light, temporarily .... But always getting back eventually.... As all attitude traps.... Frustration, worry, apathy.... All self based distortions that take us away from the truth...which is to say, away from illumination, away from pleasant intrepidness of time and mind... As all is understood, as reasons are known, and everything happens for a higher reason, and we have more to be grateful for than we see.... These perspectives are the groundwork for going beyond attitude traps...

We go beyond, in many aspects through life.... we can change our perspective to one that is more existential... or transcendental, and bypass a lot of downward / backward sliding.

It happens most often in meditation... Meditation on opening up to the infinite, or going within.... reflect on how one might see a higher perspective. To cut beyond, realize in meditation that all life is external distraction... See past it, release self imposed limitations.... conscious walking, or a walking mindfulness can cognize all new perspectives...but the sitting setting is best....

But if one resigns to the mundane parameters and allows their finite minds, their self imposed limitations of self only, their self encapsulated illusion of a never ending, dreaming mind, to be all there is.... As a complete intelligence... Then they have too much denial of the infinite within... And too much laziness to think of the how to unlock it... And can't be cognizant of it... And are sign sealed and delivered to tomorrow..., as if today doesn't even exist.... Which it doesn't...

Hence the importance for imagination ...imagining real existence ... Entity hood... The source, the light, the genetic, the guide, the soul...5 visualization/meditations one need to hold and build upon and realize and pioneer endlessly.... just imagining a guide... You can logically deduce what one would say... And just fill in the blanks.... And walla! ... An imaginary, personal intelligence consultant.... Walking with you all day long. Watch out for negative nelly... If it feels out or off a bit... Discard it... Put a negative nellie on the other shoulder and use the counter guide to triangulate the highest logic!

Like if your feeling stressed or apathetic, give it the finger... That perspective comes from craptown...literally... There is another perspective, always.... Just visit logicville, where everything's got reason for being, stop by grateful springs, and be sure to check out faith village.... where everybody knows god's in the place!

Hummmm...
A transcendental reality just past our minds awareness... Yet with in...Always interacting.... And if we visualize it.... It becomes an ever-morphing vision to manifest in reality.
Until we can't deny it's truth.

Till we can start to conceive an infinity within.... faster than light, conspiring from love.....things will remain the same....for life.

7...The Removal

Today's topic..... Ego Dropping.
A much needed and overdue discarding.

Only we, ourselves can do it, and must... Or else... We might have to die while still clinging on to it...messy.

Joking... But everyone must someday, per se'... What if it were important to do it now?

The topic is so vast and void... It almost can't be conceived by most...unless talking about making someone feel worthless.

But if I could simplify.... It is a false concept at our foundation that need adjustment of perspective...those of being separate and alone.

As ego never dies... It's indestructible at its core...as it is the entity/ monad unit or formless being. But as a concept of alone, a strive for self, and a full of __it, idiot....

This part should be destroyed as quickly as possible...and should be easily recognizable!

We all build ego together , from childhood... Were all of the same conditioning project... So were all in checks and balance with each other.... Even the bully types, know and play by the rules of engagement in regards to bullying.... Most of the time... wish they would just be friends...as we are mostly soulful, naturally cool, and kind... pretty righteous!... But what gets in the way is doing on to, as wished back, all the time, since day one, to everyone... the orientation we develop is stemming from how distorted we form our self concepts, in regards to others.... siblings, TV hero's,,, Usually we mimic what we see.. But I don't want to get into stuff like, harsh parents, and the raisin of kids they be doin'.... I mean you and me... simple kids... Empty and finite as hell...and having read transcendental stories from the ancients...thus, potential for recognitions of these sorts..

How to drop the ego?

Starts with letting go of past notions and concepts of normal self-hood... Nothing to invalidate... Just natural selfhood In the 3rd dimension...all it has known, felt, seen.... Put aside temporally ..... and embracing a vision of pure emptiness, as your self imposed removal.

From someone to no-one...

You are an idea.... A thought.... In between 2 things... 1 is DNA... 2 is The Source of Consciousness.... You are neither of these two things.... Yet you use these two things as if they are yours and as if they Are You!

Funny.... I don't recall maintaining genetic health while providing consciousness awareness intelligence to every molecule...

Hummmm...
Something missing here.... Me?... There is none... I am formless, emptiness, nothingness... Just an idea.... And a conceptual frame-work to reinforce that idea...that framework is not only flimsy as hell.... It's built on many falsities....

You are a living legend stuck in a living lie.... The ego struggle.... The self-loathing it can cause... The inescapable torture of self kept in, and allowed to bondage of self.

In many regards self is the definition of selfish, but not always... Self is mostly concerned for friends and family very quite well...it is the notion, feeling, and delusion of alone and separate that are the foundation of ego's problems...causing it to fall away into self based, and self encapsulated distortions.

Ego exists after death of ego, just more justified!

But if one takes face value for life.... They become fools led by their noses,.. Just because they never knew how to drop it. Stop the illusion machine in its tracks...keep stopping it even after it's dropped! ... Forever, till there truly is none....

Unity in place becomes in effect... notions of selfhood long slain.... and you become a node.... A unit of light for truth transmissions.

Remember, between your body, and mind, lies you... That pure nothing... The empty mind... You don't exist! Don't try to exist either, just let go! ...As you are already empty!.... Aka: ... Unified with the formless.... nothingness....(some books say we never left the after death plane...as a side note.... At the soul level)....Ya gotta build up an ego in order to have one to drop... Once built.... Needs truth adjustment...needs to die, as it is a lie.... It contradicts the unity and importance of sharing of your soul with others. Truth preservation needs notions of alone and separate dropped in order to preserve real truth...that your soul is genuine and sincere to love for totality, and can't veer from that fact... Which is to say your choosing to surrender to the unity.... And drop the opposite.
And thus no longer needs to learn this lesson... As it saved it's self by dropping it's false definition of self.... the one it was taught in school.. The lie!

And embracing the real, formless, egoless, alert, aware, simple consciousness, as sum total, of a microcosm of totality.... an entity, or a soul.

Once you realize you are nothing and don't exist... Just an empty void inside your mind ...you may die, grasshopper...
The conscious mind will know...The genetic and the etheric ARE the illusion called your body and mind... And you... were never here at all.... Just an empty thought waiting for this opportunity to

symbolically die.

Poof!

Somewhere between all that blood and guts, and endless mental conceptual activity... Is the actual you.....

Real light!

8.....Meditation

I feel like reflecting on meditation... Sumthin' we all ought, a lot more of...
The big reason we don't is that we don't have time, energy , reason enough to do it, or motivation, or belief there's sumthin' in it fer us worth our while.

But if put in simplest terms it is easy and important!
It is as simple as 7 seconds a day... One big breath... And just close yer eyes.   It breaks the arrow that flies by day into 2! It resets the day, and the now... It clears the mind, it stops time, it aligns with higher self, it makes a new moment where there was a continuance. If your ever stressed, just close for one breath , and it's less than half overwhelming... It re-empowers us! Rejuvenates, resets, & reminds us! It is the way, young grasshopper.

Try to turn it into 7 minutes a day...you'll find after three weeks there will be a noticeable change... Just meditate on nothing... nothing the concept, just anything, or nothing at all, or real nothing... Meaning more devoid of content than the concept will allow, while still being able to be considered a concept at all!

 Meditate with eyes open, closed, walking, lying, in chair, thinking, not thinking, listening, visualizing, moving awareness around from head to toes, repeating a mantra, or a positive affirmation... After a thousand repetitions... do breathing calisthenics ... Try agh, ahh , ohh, hee, haa, hoo, huu,...etc., breath slow, breath fast, fall out your nose when you breath out, Get sucked into a black hole when you breath in, tune into the small, cellular, or big, like the sky, get awake, alert, quiescent , alive but not active, flowing in place...

Get static, or ecstatic , or illuminated, or revelatory , or cognitive, or perceptive, or imaginarily, or slow, and free... just natural!

Anything goes! ...Just do it patternistically.. Religiously,,, as it is eventually gonna lead to finding inside stuff... Which is divinity...

If it becomes a pattern it's like a normal part of life...automatic ..., there's millions of reasons to do it, millions of ways to do it! :)

Please, for me,., once you get past the newness of the daily ritual... It simply integrates into already established patterns of the day... You will find resistance at first; it's the downward pull opposing enlightenment.... It's trying to deny to your true nature, trying to keep you trapped a mundane pattern, an ego limited, a non-with in...Within your own self!

Turns out this weird truth is, that god has been trying to awaken everyone all along, but no one knew how to listen...how to hear... and those who did, couldn't interpret what the silence was saying.... but with the mighty power of logic... we can deduce that god is real, god is of love, god is in the house, and that god loves to share...

You deserve it... It is inside you,,, thus, it's yours... Take it back!.... Just push on through... Just close your eyes, and take one breath....

Symbolically speaking, to close eyes, is like letting go of the outside world... To the with-in, and one breath is like becoming one with the empty essence that is source, like the one breath, one movement that is sourcing the now everywhere at once!

I want to hear after 21 days that you put in 7 min a day towards consciousness enhancement... Trust me it works... But you'll notice nothing for a while... but then you'll start to be let in a little, and you'll eventually become a meditation junkie, as you can truly move through mind/time/and other stuff only when cut off from external distraction.

See the time flow of a day forces us to go go go, outside world stuff.. While thinkin' a lot... But that's mostly very conceptual, not intimately listening to within, which is needed to grow mentally better than we have been,,,

Were all in the mundane sludge ...
... The quagmire...

And denial of its drag really puts this process on hold....I wish I'd meditated more... Lazy to live content, with no reason to go beyond... And these shoulda been faced, as we knew all about it, and It's not easy info/ perspectives to come by....No eternal reward will forgive us now, for wasting the day... Sort of speak.

Do it ... Do it for me, for you, for your soul, for your source, for your guide, for your DNA, for your lovelight inside.

Meditation is the key.... The mystical link to the unknowns.
It's poetry in motion, it's prophetic, it's enlightened, it's respect and tribute to the everything we take for granted, it's overdue soultime, it's a calling to all... Come on in… if ya think ya can...
... so whadda ya think, think yer worthy enough to get in?

Say yes.... It's birthright! It's the true you, and nature of mind, and body, spirit, and soul... Which brings us to tomorrow's topic... Spirit!;)

9.....Spirit

Spirit moves in all things!

Vibratory rates of atoms IS the movement of movement itself.
We have a spirit as an entity... but I feel it is something other than personal.... Spirit is connected to Great Spirit inseparably, which is why it's so confusing why some strive for self....

 Is it because they never knew there was a choice, to be in with the unity above, or to stand-alone?

Spirit seems to be fast, and very alert, yet somehow of consciousness of it's own, and very close to the source... Like a creation of source to nurture us... Light, and spirit are like creative principles... Which are at essence feminine.... Like mother nature... Spirit is the transcendental and the mundane simultaneously. It is like an overseer,... and the quest drive with in us, to find spirit.

A fun perspective is to put a "spirit of" to anything.... The Spirit of Christmas, for example, has a life of it's own... If you want it to,... it's like an essence, a vibe, a feeling, a certain special something to some thing... Like a favorite band, there is a spirit of the whole band as a whole... And at a concert, or in a car, yer with it, immersed within it... Becoming one with it's increasing meaningfulness.... and the meanings still unheard....the spiritual messages cloaked within.
Put a "spirit of" to driving, showering, eating, sleeping, dreaming, waking up, brushing your teeth... Ok, but really... in meditation,or being at work... put spirit in...It's up to us to do... Or emptiness will prevail. With recognition, of the realization....we can find spirit. Spirit is big everywhere, much smaller in me, yet bigger than I think.... Meditate on this reflection...Increase its meaningfulness.... Indefinitely.

Spirit is patiently waiting for our recognition, and our sweet surrender:)

One must let go of the mundane to be renewed in the transcendental.....
Ya don't want to be empty, ya gotta have spirit;)

I don't have as much ability to deduce spirit because I have so much yet to discover, and It seems to be a very slippery and vast mysticism. But I do know it has a lot to do with spontaneity, and confidence.

And imagine everything having a spirit of... Your car, your tooth brush, etc... As they do know their function, even at the level of inanimate matter....at the molecules themselves.

It is the movement of grace, in the most unimaginable display:)

Spirit is one of the great unknowns, and a never ending quest...
One of many, ...all of which are equally important to piecing together the big picture:)

Side note.... I just made a recognition....
Spirit in big terms... On 3rd... Like a daycare.... On4th... It is at separate between two orientations... Yet it is not divided with in itself... So I wondered how the unity works to separate, and it occurred how a spirit would be able to walk through walls... I already know about the fact that spirit matter is 4th dimensional at it's essence... Which means, the sub atomic molecular universe itself is the spirit... And it's even more magnificent on the 5th dimension, free from molecular bonds, in a reality plane of light...Spirit's native state.... This is how come the negative nelies are considered soulless. ...They no longer have potential they did in third... Now they have no limitless access potential ... No different from 3rd... Only with no potential for going within, for infinity.... Still remain finite ego locked , enhanced, of course, but still, they don't share minds, they are more or less just thinking beings..... With no hook up from the source...
Who is of Love... It's proven, trust me...The unity is only for the sharers...Spirit can range from etheric mutable...To empty shell. Hummmm....
Very interesting.

10.....Arrival

I see a vast amount of nothing.... Ever increasing, and diluting any "thing" to almost, basically nothing.
Best put.... Finite shrinks, and dissipates with time... combo of short term memory, and natural propensity of time... So all I put in, seems to get sucked into a vacuum ... To no avail,,,
Ever feel the same way? ... That's where the permanency of memory, and temporariness of time, split.
One must believe in the permanent database in soul memory...
Not long term brain memories, but to that which remains after death of the physical.... Soul conspires due to elder's rules for even stage....
So try to make this more real, hold on, and own it.....a love like this

should not fade away.... Just because of a universal, age-old thing called illusion locked... Ego pending to drop... Still building up from adolescence.... Never thought it could be adjusted.... We hold in our now mind a power of recognition, and realization... We can unlock the illusion... We must believe we can... It is inside us... We are it!

Don't let the never-ending finite black hole of time suck all this away from you.... Use the gifts, recognize their rareness, power, logic, and opportunity... Don't doubt it. Don't let it pass you by, just because you didn't believe in yourself transcendentally... Your true self... The timeless side, that senses that this could all be true, ...

You can do it! ...I believe this... you have the right to, as well. But don't get frustrated or caught up wanting it....Or not wanting it... Positive expectation it will happen, ...and it will...young grass-hopper.

That's faith in action.

I did it... All it took was belief, reading good stuff, thinking and connecting the dots, and a dedicated dedication to getting dead ego-wise... And enlightened, and awakened, and to meet the truth... through meditation for three weeks is all I've ever done to go beyond, but now, or since... I can occupy at any moment a piece of mind with a creative power...an ability to close my eyes and create!

You'll get to speak from experience of trying.... Not ever about at-tainment, as all's already in place.... It's about acknowledging and recognizing god, and adjusting self-concept accordingly....
You know about the invisible presence...and like all challenges to genius's... Just turn it into a game, which you will master!

Sidenote....... Your right there....Your ready and on point...full of potential, ignitable, vibrating at your own unique signature,... An eye that is as an AM. Your soul is the dreamer, and you are the dream,... if your mind can fade away, then let it. ...your light is shining bright...

.... your bio-computer's operating system is divine by nature, very efficient, built to assimilate existence...Knows how to know because it's directly connected to the divine programmers...and has light electricity flowin' in it's circuits .... All the time!:)

11.....Meeting And Reaching

I wonder if I'm going to ever get to thee other side of all this endless rhetoric... And find the Light.
It takes a level of sincerity rarely seen... A dedication mindset that is set, and a desire to acknowledge the truth... You got these ... I do too... But it takes all three to be held in consciousness for like an hour to have a change,

It seems we have to make it happen, not wait... yet, one must do nothing, and wait, at the same time...or interval both,... put energy in to get it back... it's hard.

It takes monks years... of super dedication, but here in the west were graded on a curve, so we can still be a bit lazy, and aloof about it... but ya still got a show em' you hear it, care, and believe in working with the calling, that has fallen on you.

Recognize the love that flows.... Follow it, and don't let go... and it will grow:)

There is a driving mechanism in us that keeps us pushing on to better and expand ourselves... Some listen to it better, but we all have it... And some fall deaf to it... Apathy, for example, is a decision to die, slowly, in denial of all there is to live for,... unless it's from really bad stuff... then one needs a softer pep talk.
We will know the true nature of everything after death in a 4th dimensional life, but in third, we need to wake up to the positive divine... As there is a negative side... and higher thought pending a maturity of mind.

Otherwise you can see where you and your life will go indefinitely ... Paternalistically, comfy, with a perch with in your self, private, separate....a king.

Who would want to give that up?....
Sacrifice self for greater whole?...
Oh, well, guess there must be nothing we need to realize, or any big deal, since no one else cares to know, or knows, or cares? To seek the final insight... The ultimate truth.... So important, existentially... to show yer maker your well crafted in your intelligence endowment... Logic plus!
No dummy, no fool, no pansy, doubter, lazy lover of an empty, typical, dime a dozen mind.... stupid shmow.

I unfortunately denied enlightening stuff like source vision, as very important... the result... lazy and dumb... Potential taken lightly, superficially, nonchalant, whatevery.... Where's the sincerity? The passion? The logic... Not in my recognition ... We need reminders, from friends, music, and books...or we fall away.... Like None of it ever mattered....Why? Because of doubt?

How hard can god really make it?
...Impossible?
Yes, absolutely, but don't let that little challenge distract you.
I feel your exhaustion, and frustration.... vibes of like, "you can't do anything ... You don't need this."

But really.... do you see anything potential-wise, practical, and able?
Of course, but really...really, really.... Do you believe you can meet and reach these?...
Simply not disbelieving, upon hearing it... is the key.•)

12.....The Holographic Blueprint

The holographic blueprint theory is a fun one. It makes reality nothing more than light play....

It says basically that none of this exists.... this book, the words, your hands...etc.

It comes from inside our heads first, and shines back at us faster than the "speed of light"... It shines on a 3D blueprint of every-

thing, and seems real, just enough to fool the masses..
But it's just a temporary expression of molecular energy.. A symbol... An idea...
A meaningful part of all the meanings of life.

Trying to get us past where we are.. To where it's meaning is designed to take us... To our souls, and the stars.

We all have a flashlight in our heads... It strobes... Time itself... It's like headlights of a car... And where they point they shine brightly... And illuminate stuff, or shed light upon things.... And everything behind you is black and empty!

Till you turn your head... Trust me you'll break your neck trying to catch it in a lie...
So, each step you take... Onto an empty void... The mirror of consciousness becomes floor, just beneath our feet the micro second we hit the blueprint... Driving on air... In many regards.... The hologram also applies to us... Empty inside... hallow.... Just a holographic potential for things, with a karmic signature...In theory.

We can transcend anything if we believe enough... It's sleeping in our genes ... Hard to believe, I know... Nonetheless.... Things are more than meets the eye... This can become seeing things for how they really are.... and become finding the truth right in front of your face...to maybe tumbling right out ones eye! (joke)

Visualize seeing visions... picture reality dropping the illusion lock.... Simple as a reversal of perspective... All is light!... All is temporary illusion of thought!

13.....Sacred

Well... I see a need for some diggin' into the word sacred.

There is such a thing, I believe.... Somewhere... there has to be.... Could nothing be sacred? Could emptiness be sacred? It's closest to formlessness of source...
Could a concept, or a belief in god be?

Maybe we need to define it a bit.... It's... Most meaningful?....
That's it?... Darn, I wanted something lord of the rings like....
Something so mystical, oh yea, that's what arrival to reaching the
truth is all about... To know the unknown?
What is sacred and does it matter?... Yes, obviously, but what and
why are deceptive.
So I will make my everything important sacred...
... People try to hold a belief about notions of god as sacred.... too
empty and conceptual for me....Just thoughts, ideas, concepts...
It's somewhere though... It's seeing the light... Moments of clar-
ity.... breakthroughs...
But what is it were looking fir?... Sumthin' sacred we can wor-
ship... Hummm.... It's enlightenment ...Awakening.... Sparking...
Forming... Becoming one with what were already at one with, The
Light.
We need to manifest the passion vision, in us, of the sacred....
We need to make the sacred real, and listen for it in our lives.

But first we need to really define just what is sacred to us...

Nothingness is close... the peacefulness... The freedom from
thing... The space to move... Sounds nice, but I need something
more substantial than emptiness...

Sacred waits and weeps locked away, less than a centimeter from
you.... Behind your awareness... Inside you.

I am one with source... Truth is sacred, light is sacred, spirit is so
noble, so ancient, so real, so everywhere around me, and inside,
with no separation between the two.... It's sacred!

If one really settles down into the word.... Really grasp it's depth
for how it appropriately should be seen... Finding, holding, and being rapt in awe about.... The formless divine within, as sacred...

It's merely appreciation, and inspiration at the highest levels. ...A
faith reinforcement.

And it's a sincerity within one, that matches the truth of how much
one seeks, and realizes The Truth......Simply put.·}

14.....Attitudes

The truth of attitude states... Nothing can affect one...just ones own attitude....

... Ouch!

Some of it's gotta be someone else's fault?.... No?
All mine?

...What!

It's true.... Somehow... It's all in us, and up to us, and under us! We are king of self in now!
Frustrated, pissed, ticked off, annoyed, sick of, had enough of, want out of, worried about, depressed about...

All attitudes that are our own fault...
...hurts donut?

Well, the problem is reacting... We all find 20/20hindsight always emerges,,, and shows no need for the stance... That stance was handled out of less perspective, than is seen after the fact...
Always how it is... With every time we lower to an apathetic view, get mad, or worry bout sumthin'...

We need to remember and spot it.... When ticked,,, remember... That's it ... The attitude trap... Stop it in it's tracks! ... Been down there before... saw how it ended up... Felt stupid for reacting in attitude stance....

But the overwhelming feeling frustration, worry, and depression bring... How to just say no...
"calm blue ocean, calm blue ocean, calm blue ocean"...

We can stop the negativity with recognition of the positive!
Instead of always letting stuff of the world pull us down...

Which brings us to our next topic....
Gravity!

15.....Gravity

Gravity, surprisingly originates in our souls!
It is the desires for this three dimensional level to satisfy/teach our soul, but how can it be all there really is, when our soul is limitless in it's potential... Thus we see this plane is for beginners...
Now, there is the effect we see in the outside world... Stuff drops.... But the real solidification came when the desires of self-hood stopped learning and strove for themselves in the form of selfish desire... And existential frustration set in... Yet we continued to strive, wouldn't recognize the contradiction to unity, and let go... We demanded this reality serve us! Because we thought we were only self's, were forever limited to a third dimensional construct...were supposed to achieve some sort of dynasty or permanent thing, here... To possess and control ... So we could be kings forever...
Ego... The delusion of selfhood... Is the glue of gravity... Here to serve our desire for some thing...
Can we existentially let go... And release the illusion lock...
It is the non-positive attitudes that solidify finiteness... The positive ones free up, and expand space, and insight.
Ones like, jealousies, greed, hate, apathy, and fear...
Trapped in time isn't so bad with out all those things that make it constricting as a meat grinder....

We don't need the third dimension... It's simplistic for lazy souls... drop it, as a notion of all there is;)
No one knew there was a fourth... Where real reality begins.. This is fake by definition.... A static symbolic reality of empty concepts and dead patterns.
Look to the real, the new, and the unseen, ... Only we can do it, it's up to us to want to, to see the logic to… to believe in the transcendental essence surrounding within and out... Believe in making the truth of soul real…. based on my logic… It's gotta be real... It keeps pressing for me to wake up.
Realize all I am, am not, and how others are.

Levitation, telekinesis, out of body experiences, astral projection, formlessness,... These are cool things directly involved with gravity...more graduated...

Like how molecular bonds are linked to mind, and can be affected ... Changed or broken by powers in mind... Alchemy? Shape shifting? Too heavy for me... I work with subtleties ...that can be easily overlooked... and are universally relatable... like attitudes., emptiness of mind and time.. Selfishness vs. not so selfish... These are gravity related locks...ego related.... illusion related.

If we desire things of the world.... Finite limits are sure to bog... This is the big catch twenty two...chasing shadows on the cave walls... Keeps us in bondage of a hive-like mentality, and a thingyness limitation.
We must let go of thing want, tougher done than said,... but not to deprive use of,... just desire for...we must let go of wants of the objective world... While still pushing on towards what we want... We must see this tiny , symbolic world of temporary molecular expressions of energy... That inevitably ceases for each.. That leaves everyone feeling empty, and ailing in the end... never really existed.... Just a temporary illusion... Of self's desire to not go beyond illusion level... But to hide in it, cherish it, and pretend like it's very satisfying and all you really need.

The paradox here is simple. Shouldn't desire things of the objective world... but must desire in order to achieve.... Joy, balance, & enlightenment takes much desire to attain... But not self based desire...motive selfless.... can you figure it out.... Emotional energy put in, from the heart, equals ones sincerity level...
It's the secret to dropping self focused stances.... love for others is always increasable, and is a potent counter measure to everything that can bog us down.

We are already existent at the fourth dimensional level.... The soul is of that plane always.... Consulting with elders face to face. We can move towards this vision.
Gravity free on the inside... while still trapped in time, on the out. But only as much as you keep an eye on the world going past your window.
Free from the downward pull's reach....

Ever rising up! ... Naturally!

16.....Clear The Mind

Clearing of the head is something you can choose to do or not, it's not a mandatory vision, nor vital.... Just an overgeneralized starting point...something that people can chew on to get started... One guy suggests.. Turning the self you know into a perspective of neurotic, fake, and ego driven... dropped easily... Others lean towards friendly and comfy, very self-validating.... I personally was shootin' for how to be empty... Because I had put so much emphasis on it as an existential end all, and a simplistic cure all... Good old nothingness.... As a symbolic ceasing of the me pattern... But relax.... Any posture... enternal and internal.... But if you try to hold someone else with you... DNA, guide guy, light woman, source.... your not as prone to day dream...
Try to relax to let the alpha wave flow... Voidness is simple and very interesting.... Your inside eyelids are the movie screen... And your blood moving through your capillaries, in yer lids can create the strobe, or flicker needed for imagination and dream ability to spontaneously create!

Let go, let it take you where it will, go with the flow,,,, eventually to surrender to it!

... 7 min a day.... You and the light ...unify .•}

17.....Negativity

Personally.... I don't like to think about negativity, or it's per porters...But if one want's to believe in a continuance after death, an old soul guiding, and a graduation to an ancient...then there is a potential for an opposite to good guidance... a non good soul.

Patience.... Nothing really matters except unconditional love... Being slave to others reluctance to unlock their illusion...
Maturity comes from necessity to put up with a daycare of a world for others sake more than your own...
Saint service... labor of love... proving ground for truth preservation.... endurance challenge, the learning process of doing onto even when not done back on to.

I wonder if it is ever easy, ...it must just be slow to be recognizable... Similar to how long it takes children to grow up, or so it seems, ...I think it must have something to do with a virtual infinity of data base inside.. in the brain and mind... It simply takes that long to process and update every file... Seems like a slow computer, but it's cranking as fast as it can all the time.... It really just takes ridiculously too long for anyone to wake up, realize anything, and be able to add one plus one...
 especially as far as connecting the dots of the puzzle of mind, brain, soul, god, nature, elders.

So, if there is a guide.....could there be a counter guide?

Could there be a force working against us moving forward....
Keeping us dumb?   Persuading, ... and tricking us into begetting a fondness for stupidity?
Pulling the wool over our eyes? Lying, misdirecting, deceiving?
That confounded downward pull is at it again!

You Bastards!

May I introduce you to your own worst enemy? ...
His name is Devlin....   (rhetorical humor)

There are multiple levels of negativity... Most that we will be dealing with are subtle and basically harmless... We don't need to address anything more negative....

There is a native opposite spin to god... It is as silent and as present... It is our own natural propensity towards selfishness.. And it is the major cause of laziness, arrogance, and carelessness.
Our personal procrastinator.
And it is the negative attitude enhancer. It works insecurities, self-doubt, the self-imposed limitations...
Basically it's a good game in sucky form...Leads people to realize the importance of the golden rule, and love... The natural counterpart to good, progressive movement. .... aka ego self...lower self...or, the aspect of mind that truly wants to be separate, within the unity.

Now enter the 4th dimensional entity of negativity, the counter-guide...The spiritual advisor for lies, the master of deception, the anti-truth salesman. He consults ones soul or subconscious all the time.... Almost anything you think can be considered a request for advisement from him.... Based on how much we buy into his crap, and how likeminded we are, determines how many resources he assigns to us... His goal.... mess em' up!... And keep em down as long as possible...And he has....And we're to blame.... We did it ourselves... We chose to get mad, get depressed, get scared.... Bad attitude decisions/lessons facilitated all downward travels...Selfish thinking is relative ... To what's selfish to who you know...to a point.

Our souls laziness, and reluctance to wake up... Our existential undecidedment... The polarization to service minded is tough... There's a lot of drain on one.
Everyone will be used as a tool to frustrate you... You will be challenged and fail. But recognition of where it comes from allows you to assign blame accordingly, give him the finger, and not give him those precious rewards anymore.

Can't get mad, sad, or scared evermore! Or at least very quickly and then return to normal.
Devlin's got your number.... Knows your weaknesses, and will strike when least expecting…
On guard!....
Carry the shield of love!...(hold the recognition, and you can't veer!)

We are going to know the opposition to good, always. It is our gauge for good.... It is a never-ending challenge because there is always new angles on the lesson of selflessness... And others are always puppet-able and non-cognizant.
So, the service to self is a never-ending lesson while here... We must be ready at all times.... As we can slip in an instant... Get upset, squeezed, or loose steam at many points a day.
New definition to walking on thin ice....
The downward pull has a heat gun...
But we supply the energy....
...Cut em' off!

18.....Meditative Visions

Today we have... more meditative visions....

The visualization facility is waiting in everyone.... Very few find it's potential, sitting quietly in our heads all along.... I found I could picture anything.... My best friends face... Walla... There It is!....

Same with songs.... A picture of each thing they say.... Making a morphing music video as the song unfolds...and different each time!
Archetypal essences, I call em'. ...Forms of things and people... Mentally visualized...
We all have them of every one and thing ever seen or imagined... This Is the entry to recognizing the lights creative principle in us... as it can become visions... Two eyes looking at everything you look at... The light and you..,. Actually like five eyes.... in an intimate listening, and story telling relationship.
You can work with it, and put in, or just sit back and listen.
.... All one has to do is just close their eyes and imagine something like seagulls, flapping in a clear distant sky......Set's a vision for visualization!...You can imagine them.... See them! Put them in motion, and know they will always be in there, flying around in your head, any time you want!
Your light is sleeping, kind of... lazily conspiring, ...But it can create thousands of images per second.... In real time motion... Aka ...lucid dreaming!....
Going within is something you make up! .... Anything goes... Imagine a door.... Imagine you can open it and step through it.:) Imagine an optic fusion embrace!
Just listen to your breath Go in go out, and get sucked into that massive black hole called a nose... then fall out like a waterfall.... Repeat a series of words like..."light, void, mystic, flow"...or stretch it..."the light, the love, the seed, and the source" over and over, until you can't anymore, and tell me how you feel;).Imagine a dissipation of mind that really ceases to exist...imagine walking down a series of stairs, imagine opening a door to find another door indefinitely... Imagine dissipating physically, to become the un-formed, what it means to get formed.... to get sparked...to turn up

your love light for people you admire... for the world...
Imagine your sitting on an infinite unconscious underneath you that your merely the tip of the iceberg thereof, and you can slip down and swim limitlessly within straight down, imagine seeing your arterial network from an inner tube raft of a red blood cell, to float downstream on... And imagine what the journey would look like from there...imagine love showering/ misting on you from the light... light information packets being sent to you from your DNA, your spirit guide, super old entities at the council, the source... Liquid light, static light, hazy light, clear light...Imagine the source within, shining so bright, that you can scarcely stand to look at it. Imagine your internal living room...where everything is life size.... Imagine a longer now...going within every second, faster than the speed of light, into an infinite data base, and back to the surface in under a second.... And imagine it continuing 24/7... It was stated Einstein built a watch in his mind ... with gears and in motion...inventors building it first in mind, then in the physical world.

It's a personal limitless infinite potential... Birthright deprived... We are more!
There is a lot of potential ...to our native nothingness...from nothing comes something... The voidness is recognizable in it's spherical multi-ability.... Like as simple as reading a street sign while watching the road too.. Or to be aware of a person talking and listening to the TV as well...
Remember everything we see is a projection of light onto the back of the head... Traveling down the optic nerve tube.... Till it strobes it's crystal illusion across your membrane of a movie screen.
All is merely potentiality for voidness.... Nothing is, as it seems.... Everything's alive! .... It all knows its function! Consciousness is everywhere.... Nowhere is it not.... Much more to everything than meets the eye...
More to DNA, more to the guide, more to the deceptions, the source, the light, a spirit, a soul, a you, than meets the eye!
Much, much more, and will be as well, on evermore.

And the healing potential... mentally, subconsciously, and physically can and do occur in a meditative state... one place one can get out of time and be in a fresh space, for anew....And since calling to the divine for self help is tricky.... It provides them opportunity time to work with us... Conscious style.

It's probably the most important thing anyone can do... Most good
for mind, body, soul...and very powerful, and satisfying.... and
needed....

It's vital... It's the secret key to freedom we all had the whole time
... Just close the eyelids and see the world more clearly... Go
within... It's limitless, multi-void, enlightened, mature, accomplished, wise, and hip,,..

It's a really mystical thing.... Cloaked... Right beneath everyone's
noses, the whole while;)

19.....Word Meanings

Metaphoric wordage like the light and spiritual can seem fluffy and
dead.
They are only symbols of a greater reality that

Only the mystics of ole' knew... But we can know... because it has
survived the test of time... is here with us,.... just as it was with
them... back in the day.
Awaiting arrival of our recognition of it.
These concepts will slither too and fro in yer fro for ever... as long
as you find logic, and take em' to heart,.,, and someday... Down
whenever.... You'll start really realizing all of them...
They are all potentially real... If you believe they can, should, or
are already.

I imagine a labyrinth in our heads that holds all these potentials
as very pending... And we can start seeing these peeking back at
us... Or they can fade...If they don't seem very important.

The source is very sincere about this... No games, no dreamy
deception.... Just an honest word that it is here for you... You are
of it... And it's gotta be a challenge., or else it doesn't hold a fitting
worth.
The light is no friend of man's ego... (delusion of selfhood) but
loves us as souls eternally... The guide uses his counterpart as

tough love... Everyone falls short of true genuineness and sincerity in recognizing the sacred... But that's only proof of its truth.... the anti logic we sift through while waking up, preserving truth, and dropping notions of alone..... They have endless compassion to our plight... Also zero tolerance for our laziness, self-loathing, and bad attitude stances.
Basically our souls are cool, we're a pain in the ass.

I have had so many chances for awakening.... But faded away.... They were there for me all along...I have had opportunity, with everyone waiting on the edge of their seats about me.. And I always drifted off... Missed it.. It is working with us, unbeknownst, and unawares to us.... We have had, and lost opportunity just in the past two weeks of this....
Aloof, is a tough one....because sincerities there... But recognition strength, and realization of a big picture of it all, is tough... Spiritual bulk to mull these over to a point of completion, is accomplished, ...to say the least...
But we will always have more opportunity.... But it still holds record of prior misses....
We should try harder to wake up.. More recognition of it in sight and not to loose sight. ...Takes practice ... We need our own comfy posture... No pressure, or it looses spontaneous cool... Motive gets less than psyched.
So we need to believe with rock solid faith that we can and will arrive at realized of these self evident truths;)
Working with the unformed... is tricky at a base conceptual level... But you hear it.... They are here ... Invisibly and just allowing.... and we know this with out a doubt ... So it's only polite to acknowledge them, and kindly get to followin' this;)
Somehow...a little push on through to get into a meditative/realization/awakening/arrival pattern.
For your higher self, in tribute to god, DNA, the light, the spirit of love, the spirit of enlightenment, the spirit itself coming into your body at the solar plexus axis.
They.... whoever....seem to be the ones who decide to pull the veil... We can't really bust into transcendental terrain... It's a process of initiation.
But it's up to us... Nearly 99%! ...They know we can't do much but dream... Everyone's gauge is different and unique to our certain

circumstances... Equal employment opportunity program. Need to get serious about true selfhood, dignified, realized.... Aware of the subconscious, the super-subconscious, and brain alternately ... Aware of source presence, guide presence, evil's presence, the light's presence, and DNA's presence. Aware of where were going, supposed to be, and going to arrive at... Aware of all we are, all at once!
All these words are simply vehicles, to get us from point a, to point b... They carry meaning that carries us to a place anew, one less found, unheard of... the place where every new moment, actually is like a new moment!:)

.....It is time for reflection.... To continue like I been... Swallows up prior nuggets.... Digestion, and a sorting out is occurring in higher minds...
Try to rejuvenate refection on these thoughts...
I'll resume when Los inspirationalisms return;)
Hang loose, but tighten it up like a taper;)

20.....Realization

I think were all feeling kind of weak in the realization area.... But I think were spotting things for glimpses at a time better these days.... A source? Who'd a thunk? A light to sight? A higher self? That is separate? A deception?! A lesson,... an illusion,... an infinity ... Many infinities? A Subconscious mind? A Soulmind? The collective unconscious of earth? DNA intelligence as a friend? Super consciousness guides?

Mind senses its limits... knowing there's more, just beneath.....

Head cocks, eyebrow raises, moment pauses...and on again.... But ever so closer to the mighty recognition... The light within.

So...
The Mind is very insult able, as a lazy deaf dumb blind, arrogant self-serving, self-destroying machine.
This is aspect of ego, illusion, and karmic record...But there is another aspect.... The one that's cool, we are all down with, and

digs smiles...
And just past that is real power.... And more past that....magic.

Mind is wonderful, perfect, and amazing... Its fluidity, its silence, its neutrality... it's a self-conceiving, self-containment unit!
And it's finite, slow, and primitive...
And it doesn't exist!

Everything's conceptual... Mental subject object separation game where no one, and nothing can touch you... A naked king! In a world that is merely imaginary and mental....and transparent!

Clearly paradoxical.... Clearly needs attention, and investigation.

The mind is the vehicle for much more than we think.
Our whole mental world is held together by thoughts... With emotional weights varying... And influencing.

With the endless files in the subconscious being updated or scrapped all day/night...constantly grinding it out . The soul is more intellectual.... But the subconscious has a mind of it's own too...just a bit less knowing.
And as a conscious mind, we "think" we are all there is...we have nearly 99% control... Our thoughts precept reality.... What we think is real for us, is.... And what we think, is real for us... We dictate our future and our now with free will of mind... But we don't know the mind for it's full potential... So we keep our self's limited to pattern, simply by not recognizing pattern isn't learning anymore.

The thought energy we send out directs subatomic atoms, spirit matter.... which sculpts our days. Destinies, lessons, karma, and surprises!
One can picture how they want stuff to turn out and give positive affirmation...and visualization can bring it about.
There are messages from the subconscious... Subtle...and behind the front... the soul seems higher intelligence... Then there is non-thought... meaning, not from in yer head... From up there... Only which one...
Seriously.... Discernment should be the most important, and thought of word.... As the two opposing forces are part of this...and the unity vision gives access to greater bounty.. ..

So , how to increase mental energy to get beyond. To get motivation?... How to spark?

Mind needs to be realized, and firmly believed to be over matter!

Mind came first!

It's where it all originates!

All perception comes from within!

Reality flows forth, out your head and shines back at you!

Your king of the world.... Your world... Your microcosm! And, your room full of mirrors...

By our thoughts, beliefs, recognitions, we can be mind over matter... And through positive expectation... Arrive at the ultimate truth! Mind energy is abundant if truly sought... It is the downward pull that saps and drains.... We can take our mind as a powerful controller of all we see hear and think... And guide these reigns of the vehicle where we want!

Mind energy is of spirit matter...it is intelligent energy.

Varying karmic ally and genetically.... But all endowed with intelligence from source....Imagine an intricately organized network of complex fields of energy through out the brain... Firing on all cylinders.... All fueled from above.... And that pesky guy, Devlin, siphons from ya....The mind has ample access... It just needs to really listen… think about these meanings, and increase sincerity stance towards them. And it will grow! ....For it watches us and knows what we know;)

Try to watch your self, think about why you do your patterns, see if you can change them, fat chance, but your expanding, questioning, and pushing boundaries!

Another thing to think about... Other people.... Every time you do, their soul is alerted.... The big switchboard connects us all, and sends via the unity of consciousness instantly, always... Even with earthlings of past... Socrates, Jesus, Gandhi ,…anyone!

... Beyond life and death planes.. The soul exists, for it is of spirit matter.... Beyond life or death.. Mind is the transcendental essence within, all along…Just waiting for that moment when you see that there just might be more to this, than is meeting the eye.

If you believe this is important... The energy will be there for you....

If you're unsure.... It will flux and probably fade.

So make a decision, to believe in the power of mind it self, all

notions of self aside... Mind is a jet smooth ride!
An ancient mystical metaphysical creature of everythingness!

...What if you were to be engulfed by your own infinity!... No longer being, just allowing.•}

21.....Believe

When we think about actually breaking down the conceptual
framework that we built up as our stability piece of mind.... We see
a need to unlearn a lot we've conditioned ourselves to.
Sounds nice, but teeth can't sink in... If it ain't easy it's telling
ya naaa... I feel it ... The lazy sludge that binds and stagnates...
I know there is more, more to life, mind, me... but the bondage
won't leave... How exactly did Socrates get those damn mental
hand cuffs off?... Thought them off? Believed em' off?... He just
did it!... Sought truth of stuff relentlessly... and found it... Period! ...
No if's, and's, or but's...but there is this one little stipulation about
having to consciously die!....aka: to adjust one's foundation...
Must master art of dying, in order to experience the art of life....
God and enlightenment!!!!... can you believe it's waiting?.... does
it seem like a dead game?.... whipping dead horses?,.. Too hard?
Too extreme? Too "out there"?.....

It is.... Indeed.... impossible... Miserably so...

But still... What if?.. It was just a motion away?... And it was crazy
what you could have had, had you only believed, like I believe....
in you;)
Ok. To unlearn.... This speaks to stop, look, listen... You can tell
when it's in ego mode vs. intrepid mode... You can direct it more to
cool better than ever now that it is an easily recognizable thing....
with the recognition of the great unknown, face to face.. vs. bored,
empty, and generally on auto pilot....We will continue unabated
for ever unless we start to spot the things and thoughts that are
limiting, self belittling, doubtful, lacking love, lacking good spirits,
humble gratitude, and remembrance of love...are all red flags
now....Now that you can spot each one... dozens a day!... We can
chip away at this with persistence!..

and a firm resolve to overcome.

We will see where it takes us... And we will make it like we deserve:)

22.....Break It Down

A clearer inscription of what we need to do is simply put.... Break it down.

Everything will tell you what it means, it's up to us to connect the meanings and get to the secret surprise waiting to become real once realized!

There is a day to day mind that is lazy, a "know it all", thinks it knows all it needs to know, ego oriented, pattern-like, and is sign sealed and delivered to it's next day, which will be the same, and a next life, which will follow along similar lines.

We must break the cycle... Recognize ego-based archetypes, and reject them, and remember transcendental/real truth archetypes... and move in their direction accordingly.

Moving foreword, not just circular.

We can climb out of the cave of big, black, and empty.... And the light is just peeking.... But it's proof it's there!.... We can reach it. Though it seems out of reach... objects in mirror are closer than they appear!

Once recognized and realized to be at one, with all we speak of, a whole world opens up.. You can see everything for real, in full light of day... Out of the finite treadmill called ego born mind, and on a fast track to completion of many lessons!
To the piece of mind that's a win, win situation for everyone, every moment...here for others, with something to offer.

To arrival at your true self... A soul, sparked, formed, and graduating.

23.....Take Note

I think an important thing to do is to "take note of...."

The moments flow seamlessly.... ceaselessly.... ceasing... And it cycles.... A day in the life is all there is... as far as chances to take note....
Sleep is a place we'd all love to wake up to... But daytime can be woken up to as well... Just take note... Notice these things in the world, in yourself... And this slowly gets the recognizing abilities kickin'..
I do hear you to an imaginary extent, and it says that your having a hard time keeping up, because so much is new... and it's hard... Which it will be....Just to believe in crossing a borderline inside to the other side... And doing it all just to prove you can... it's just so impossible to do... This is because of doubt, downward pulls, and a wrong motive....
Let's work on motive.... Why do you want it? Do you not want? Are you a fool? Ya gotta want truth, light, and god.... No? Ok... Here's the deal.... You need this... This is good.... This is for you.... you are of this... Your inseparable from it.
Denial is the only excuse, denial is just empty nothingness... Which is good... But in a bad way... Sagittarius is claimed to seek the truth... Maybe it's in the astrologic...
Joking... But I do know how it goes... One just doesn't believe... Doesn't care.... Yet, still cares, and believes... But basically... "Just shut up about attaining some super fantastic from god, if you "try" enough".... I hear ya... It's same with everyone... Doubt wins, lazy sludge binds, spirit says willing but soul says... "Next time, I promise... I just want to dream and take it easy"... Which it rightly should......
But the wake up... So Nobel, so mighty, so needed, so righteous, so ecstatic, so much you could have had... But through a motive that couldn't want to serve the self but couldn't see past only serving the self, finds... They don't have much motivation.... Unless you're an ambitious service to self.... to want enlightenment is hard to find the why..." What's the point"...."I'm smart, and humbly grateful as I am"...." I wouldn't want to ask god for anything more"..."I'm not sure it's even possible"....
Why should we deny? ...We have these tools now.... We did not

always have them...Shouldn't we take them.... As very important?.... Sacred?.....Really important?.... Can't pretend it's important... Must find a reason it is important.....
Anything???
Let us reflect upon this....
It's rare, it's super intelligent, and it's mystical cool... It's only right, to the light, to your soul, to your loved ones souls... It's intelligent... gives reason to many curiosities of life and death... might be the key to getting out of self focused traps.....There are more than enough valid reasons to get to getting' this... It waits, always... It is also ready to go beyond, always... We need to acknowledge this... And pay respects to source... Wake up to holding it conceptual with you always.... And to notice how fast it always keeps being.. Unbelievably faster than man's gauge of speed of light.
Time it self.... You can eventually start to notice the moments fade into each other.... to notice time pouring out your eyes.... to see time racing into your eyes... to see the invisible magnetic fluid that is the same in everyone, and every critter... Consciousness.... Unified naturally with all other consciousness... Mirrors of it self.... We are DNA expressing its-self... Not ourselves... We are not separate.... Might as well face it... Can't escape.... Better surrender.... Don't hold notion of separate as dear.... don't put off it's dropping necessity.

There is a calling to all to step to their own entity plate, to recognize gods love, and make the meanings of life take on living meaning.•}

24.....Keep Trying

If you don't press for it,... It aint gonna just hand it over.... we can't really do anything but keep the door in sight and keep knocking on it.... Don't ever believe no ones home... their just sitting quiet in there.
So...we gotta make it happen.
We can... I cant, you can't... but just maybe we can.... It's like one of those video games with two players and the one can't move foreword unless the other guy is caught up.

048

So... Keep up!;)
We are moving.... I can give propulsion, but only as much as you are here with me....I know your like" what can I do"..... Not much, except believe this is for you ... To truly know its of light, to be of guide...of you, and for us, to create anew way... for someone after us... to pioneer further.

But it can't remain purely conceptual and amount to much.... We must gain things we can use, and share.... This is, of course, actual discovery.... You should start to expect it....Now that they have us on this fast track... The most important thing is to keep an Open mind to anew and the unheard.... The truth just past this so-called truth.

The teacher is a student of this, the student is a teacher in training, This is like a soul & spirit guide.... Guide has a guide who's just a soul....only older.....inseparable, and necessary for existence to work.

7 min a day should know where this is going... Expect the change.... No matter how small... Something you had not seen or thought before... Had you not tried to go within.
I know yer brain will show ya some movement.... However shadowy, and subtle.... I know you can tune in and be quiescence of being-ness... Alert, aware, listening to flow unfold.... in the darkly of the inner lids... Imagine stuff... Practice visualizing something... Awaken and enhance your already known mental abilities of visualization.... Breathing exercises.... Be your own guide... Self-propelling back to where you came from.... Your source!
We are forever... But this is now... Let's keep putting energy into this elemental and watch it grow:)

...PS... if your ever feeling a drag... A weight to pull to get this or anything done... Spot it... It's Devlin, I swear... It's too illogical and weird energy drain... Not right... Something's amiss... It's him or his minions.... They are the feelings like that... inhibiting, or resisting something this good?... Common' it's him!
Spotting it, you can then choose... Give him the finger... Know the light and good guide are just past the one who likes to impose.... And besides, he never chips in for gas....
Kick him out!

25.....Meditate More

With meditation,...
It depends on what factors are in play.... To be natural is ideal....
All Tao like..
But the mystical access through deep concentration can amplify
visionaries... must be proper set , and setting... Mostly feel free...
a self-liberating, liberation game.... Any posture goes... Feel the
force flow through you... It flows through everything in unison....
Remember chakra points and focus on one at a time... Give
conscious awareness to the chakra area... And activate energy
vortexes... Imagine etheric centers where vital life force energy
interchanges with body

The biggest problem with meditation.. Is finding a way to do it
that's comfy and intriguing ... Thus plenty of motivation and function... But to start... So hard... And for the most darn illusive reasons...
Hold light.... as a symbol of silence... holding static now... Which
is impossible.. There is a restlessness... people speak of trying to
clear the mind... And this is unclear to me.... What it really is or
means.... As to me ... there is no such possibility possible..... The
ceaseless flow, the countless dreams, the unavoidable memories
that tumble in.... Why try.... Just let go.... Listen.... Daydream....
But the whole while your beginning the tuning in process...
Though it will seem meaningless, pointless, a drag.... This is because of how easy it is to simply walk across that borderline, once
you have just once!
Work it like a game.... Do music on... Then off.... Eyes open.. Then
closed, and start repeating a positive word like RAMA... Means
rejoice... And let the meaning of that word sink in ever so deeper...
Then do it standing, then sitting, and then lying down.... Then do
breathing... 20ha's, 20ohms's, 20heee's, 20hoooe's....
The point, is to figure a way to make it a good game... That's
enjoyable... Then after time it unfolds naturally... Just takes continued dedication ...as with completion of most things.
Just meditate.... Every 21 days it will be a noticeable change.
It's the best gift I can suggest .. As I know it works... Just have to
find this balance between believing you can, and just trying...

Sounds easy... But is the toughest trick man has to figure.

26.....The Flow

There is a flow of life, time and consciousness.... The three are recognizably different.... Life is day to day... There is flow to traffic, cooking, talking w others... We all try to go with it, best we can... Time is big ... Dimension itself.... Renewing itself every super micro second... And then consciousness stuff is the trifecta elixir... Mind awareness... The variable unit to free will... There lies within consciousness ... The truth.... flowing and unfolding. Crystal clear.... But cloaked... Esoteric symbolism is a form of mental synapsing that requires one who hears subtleties of meanings as breadcrumbs to the secrets of existence, to find the ultimate truth... It's a skill that takes training... But to a new comer... Letting flow of consciousness unfold.... Let it take you where it will.... Recognizing flow... This is the nitty-gritty of it all, as to surrender to the flow is ultimate goal....

Where you get sucked in.... Absorbed.... enveloped within..... Unlimited field of avenues of mind... The flow is what's actually happening everywhere all the time... The seemingness of static objects, seeming permanency of the objective world... The seemingly frozen in time most minds seem to be in.... It's illusion... Flow.... Of the natural mystic is everywhere... And it's of love!

Within... And pouring over our heads.... it's inescapable... Yet eludes everyone's recognition ability.... That's it!
Recognizing the clear light and dropping self encapsulated distortions of reality.... Aka ego....
Forever...this is the key to the goal...
Take note of the subtleties of divinity's fingerprints, and put the logical gears to deduction!
It will all make sense and reveal itself naturally... With out any neurological event ...or with one..... Either way, we can recognize the truth. ... We all do already.... It's just the mystically bent who hear the whisper of an ever yet so deeper one... And the only rumored...."ultimate truth"... Wherein all things are born, live, & die all in the same moment... All the memories of earth history, from earth's perspective.... Where everything is like the clear blue sky... The multi-infinities within, and around.... the transcendental reality.

Don't sell your infinity short like so many poor saps.

We do it to ourselves.... To overcome takes spotting that your trapped in illusion of finite... And the vast truth within is far more than the silly games of operating in the outside world... You are a star in a galaxy in the universe... All in your head!.... In the end... The monad in the microcosm is just that! A light source in the universe that has just as much scope as mass!

So, knowing the end of the story should clue you in to the what to envision of your real self...
And yes your normal self is real too.... It's just less real, and a very small part of the whole.;)
And all that is required is to reach that point in meditation where you aren't being the presence "being"... But where you see an ever-unfolding foreword falling into visions...and let it take you on a journey where it will.... Similar to dreams... But you're a conscious participant!

Just must really visualize the real light in you and not let it fade away...and that constant recognition of its presence can persuade your soul to spark.. And become awakened into the mind!..

27.....Truth Lies

The place where truth lies and reality breaks.... Is so in our face all the now... But so unrecognizable... Unless you check it in comparison to these chats.

There is a "normal reality" we know.... Then coexistantly, yet separate, there is the Real Truth now awareness.

It knows all... But remains ever so "not being".... Present always... And 100 times more aware... And our soul is of that presence... Higher knowing... Yourself as a soul knows what were doing here, and wants to maximize it for you.
What amazes me is how small we are in comparison.... In this now... And how the lacking sincerity can no longer be denied.... or hidden... How much we have is known and put in our face upon

seeing and hearing yourself from its perspective... And it's...
It is soooo now... It is NOW...
Always now... It is now.
Really not down the road like you think;)
It is now!

It's such an amazing realization.. I can't express it well enough...
But it is now.
.... And we should have been long ago.

The infinite light within, which IS the fabric of reality around,
conspires consciously every minute of everyday... Faster than the
speed of light... Blocking...hinting, setting up, knocking down....
The teacher.. Always schooling.... To listen and hear it for how it
really is.... Becomes a one way ticket to illumination..... As once
the meaning train is caught ... A lot of coincidences start to occur... And we're gauged to what we think of coincidences... How
we utilize them to get the most clues to meaning we can hear.
Sound weird, but it's it.... Meaning is designed to get us to somewhere... It hints of a more real version of its self... A symbol of a
bigger, more real reality...

We all do it naturally with meaning... Create synapses and play
with free association...It is the self content one that does it lazily,
immaturely, and jokingly.... distorts meanings... But to seek the
truth.... sincerely... To think of the meanings of meanings... Relentlessly:)
That's sparked... And forming... Along with being conscientious of
polarization opportunities, and seizing them... And you will surely
be graduating....

It's harder to center focus and achieve than one thinks... Undecidedment of spiritual orientation...to be service to self or service to
others...is a very large pile to mull over... We will all fail short....
But its not achievement, as it's persistent trying.... as our polarization grade is on a curve to our past, not others!.... Sincerity is the
key!. How deep is your love?.... How much are you contentious of
others in comparison to yourself? How much do you try to recognize? To realize stuff.... Put the pieces together? Show applied
learning? How much do you really care? That's what they're
looking for first...

These should be given full attention.... But in this tribe of egos we interact with... It's hard to be soulful.

This is why it is the path less taken... The secret pathway... Right inside the heads of everyone... Conspiring actively ... And to a hard core extreme.

.. Slow down... Listen like a soft heart...and take this gift/opportunity... Like a grateful, acknowledging, servant of intelligence. Adjust your sincerity ever so much never endingly more.... And then when you get stressed or frustrated, you'll have a more realistic, and down to truth, frame of reference...and it will seem in such contradiction to your sincerity to the light... That it will fold and fall away... And will happen less and less.... As this matures... Evolves... And emancipates....

Its now in the mix;)

28.....Distortion

Damn... That's it... The distortion of truth that makes it tough to master lessons.

In my face... And the interesting part is the point where I bought in to it!... Got mad, as if I had a valid reason to get upset.

Where I made a false deduction... Though logical... it was clearly distorted due to the negative energy hallmarks that were hidden within.
I don't think arrival at anew enlightened is really that easy...But maybe it's easier than I think...
To stoically want it is too aloof, need extreme level of sincerity to face it.... It's so intense.... It is god....Infinity of anything in the now.... To be completely selfless... Looking through gods eyes... No concept of a self-separate....

... Just an eye of god.

29.....Stability

Turns out there are a lot more aspects to all this, than I thought.... One really doesn't need a lot of transcendentalism.... To be spiritual.... In fact.... Simple and normal are the norm... So let's work with that.
Spiritual stability is when your centered and aligned with neutral to positive energy ...And the more immovable you are , the more stable, and helpful to others....the more immersed in positive energy....
There is a base self-focus, which is necessary for existing as a self... Then there's everyone else...Eventually one can learn to not be self focused at all... Just here for others when with others....Remove self from the scene and you'll be a lot more extroverted.... And stable.

30.....Golden Path

I just imagined a parable, where you were the lion and I scarecrow.... obviously consumed with having a brain, not having a brain... and you ... So scared to show emotion, scared to confront so much... Yet having so many qualities of the lion... Laughing... But we are all on this golden opportunity to cut beyond normal... And go down the path less taken ... Almost as if it's been placed just for us.... And the end is this rumored wizard of consciousness we're supposed to finally see! They say he's the wizard for everyone, and that he's just a wise old man, like yoda;)
And the smoke and mirrors show he can put on...
And the giving of us our powers!
Should be a great movie/ life!.•)

31.....Soul Power

So..... Getting back in the groove is tough... So much other stuff in life drains chi and results in blocks to higher mind...And I haven't been meditating......
That's the quirky thing about this all or nothing life flux challenge...

One can see amazing things, with empirical evidence of the beyond... And go about the day all-normal, like we just forgot what we saw... We take a portion into ego strengthening, then let it go... Instead of recognizing what they just got a hint of should be carried on and built upon...but it can so readily fade... As in the normal world, most people aren't unfathomably random, their typical... And that usually means a heavy dependence on self-centeredness, and a lot of pride in it... Not a lot of peeps willing to believe in going beyond normal boundary lines...and they will all drain ya, and pull you down from this.

So,...when in Rome, just do as the masses?...Naw...... I'm dropping out!

So that I may drop in, and make a change for the better.... Existential style!

So.... dedication to meeting and reaching the truth.
And an unwavering one at that!....faith it can, and will be achieved at some noticeable level, and a firm resolve to rectify any old lingering mental patterns of; apathy, frustration, worries, or anything lower self related...A symbolic ego letting go-ness....and a firm belief in the guides unseen always around.

OK...so.... Soul power! ....Got some?.....

....Our souls have to conspire to "not be here" or seem separate from the conscious mind...Though it wants to direct the life...and wants to help and guide.. And with enlightenment available, wants to attain!
...So, if we show we are learning, it acknowledges with vibes or glimpses of the soulmind... It's reality.... Enough to show it is, and knows... But still dreamy and fading...
It seems to be about this mind hearing and figuring a way to hear soul. The trick is... soul to mind communication is made by the conscious mind reaching.... Not the soul...the soul updates in it's way ..... But we must find the soul in our own little way.
The soul is in unison to conspire with light and guides...tough but caring... Biter-sweet...not very happy with slow progression of contradictions to truth preservation.... Not a buddy or parent, but supportive and always there...

There is a self-guiding principle that is encoded in everyone to get them at completion of the lessons... To the soul.... This foreword pull, I'll call it, already knows the solution to this paradox.... We just have to have faith ... We have to question illusions... And we must tune in.

The unfoldment is always naturally occurring, a spontaneous "seeing things clearly" moment.... is a good description of the flow of time, and mind.

Just be still, and know.. Just like the walls... The furniture... The calm air.

When limited to only words... Constant word assimilation fills your inner dialogue, and conceptualization processes... But the soul, subconscious mind, the guide, the deception, the light, the source all have their own forms of communication ... ...And none are in words!

Can we hear the wordless.... The essence of form?

Let a vision of love be the focus elemental... Realize you really are loved by yourself... Soul, DNA, Light, Source, Guide/Angel... Loved by so many people of earth.. Yet how hard it is for the self to have love for the self, or the world for that matter.... In our day to day moments... So much non-love.... And to maintain recognition of this simple and overwhelmingly abundance of love from above.... Hard, to say the least.
One Love is a recognition that transcends.... Instant vision of joyous universal harmony...
Give yourself the gift of unconditional love...
As with all gifts they require appreciation ... Thus recognize gods love.. As it's never far... Always near... Closer than we think.•}
it's in your recognition ability of it!

Next is the questing and questioning ...starts the call... To the guide... And the soul gets counseled and then can update the conscious mind as to the answers.. Mostly through subtleties ... Symbols, dreams, passing thoughts... Random old reflections tumble in....all cluing into the how to hear the soul.

And then, we begin the begin of the final... Light commencement!

As tuning in is easier than pie!
The easiest part of all...just close yer eyes and check it!

But to believe in yourself.... and try....

...Impossible!

But to say I love you god! And thank you so much for creating me!

...Cake!?

And they say, love is all ya need to get enlighten-met.•)

32.....A Blade Of Grass

I'd like to share with you a vision of a blade of grass....

In 1 blade, of trillions per city block... Is trillions of cells... Each
encoded with a design and a function....
And a tiny part of a bigger plan.

The cell is made with a super high tech self replicating machine..
A cloner... And it also has these cool tubes for transporting miner-
als, organic matter in decay, and for regulating thermostat.... it
can grab a photon, or ray of light, and snatch it.... And eat it and
energize its self... Funky little critters, they are!
So in that cell is a secret little center where it receives vital life
force energy... Different from sun energy, or sugar energy... It's
the fabric of reality touching existence.
This cell has trillions of molecules and each of those has a trillion
sub atomic particles.... Each smaller level is a size differential of
like a grain of sand is to the planet... Planet to the solar system...
Solar system to the galaxy... Galaxy to the universe... Universe to
infinite multiverses...

There is a truly never-ending journey above and below.... We can
genuinely travel indefinitely smaller and smaller... Forever... And

big... To eternity... and If one takes life as a message.. You open up a dialogue potential with destiny!.. mirror infinities... within and without!

The events... Emotions... Mental workings.. All speak a deeper message, if one digs a bit.

The Celestine prophecy spoke of coming into
Insights ... That build upon one another and lead to lethargic epiphanies...
These are interwoven with coincidences that occur... And the guy sometimes can recognize them and others, he cant... But when heard as a message... It's meaning propels the individual foreword to a higher awareness field..

It's god working with us... All of us... All day long.... all night long.... Everyday.... For lifetimes!
It is this matter of non-recognition that leaves it in non-existence.

Don't you hate not being acknowledged for things you do for others?

Our lives speak with symbols.. It is our message, and guidance.

Every happening, each thought... Each pattern is sayin' a lot more than we hear.... And they are a message from the higher self/ guides... Events happening for bigger than we know, because the scheme of things can see for so many miles into the future... And the rest is totally predictable to follow along established lines.

Even chapped lips are a message from the soul…the song that just came on the radio…the remembering of stuff you gotta get done….all messages.

They have been trying to get us in for years... Setting up settings with opportunity... Just because we missed it , doesn't negate the fact it was!
It's a time flow elevator ... Straight to the top!... If you can catch the ride. The flow, and hold on.... It will take us all the way….to the soul.

And it all starts with a random moment in time noticing something It had not before, something interesting and enigmatic, a blatant coincidence... The moment's set... Recognition of it, is first....Reflection on meanings flood....Logic connects a synapse or two... And one thing leads to another!:)

Holding on is so hard at first... It fades, in order to teach one to listen up ever so much more. One can meditate and have a mind-blowing experience and open the eyes, and go about dealings scarcely reflecting in what just occurred. It's laziness of ego that says," I got it good enough," "I'll think about that more later," but forgets...But to stick with it for about an hour! ... May result in amazing grace?!... I'm not sure?;)...

Could it come down to holding truth preservation to recognition for a certain duration...
One just long enough to be tough... But short enough to reach.

"... The hour I first believed...Amazing grace!

So, as you walk through time... Take note... That there is always someone trying to tell you something.... Hearing from a multi perspective ability is with in our consciousness's vastly void potential.

All just symbolic expressions of bigger symbols.•}
...Indefinitely!:)

33.....The Final Realization

The more we think about these things the closer we get to the final realization of all we know/believe.
I have been working in it for 20 years now... And have come full cycle enough to see how slow this can go... But it never ceases… it can only build!:)
But it could have propelled years ago into manifest, had I dedicated to believing I could, that I am assisted, and am expected to arrive by the assisters!

There is a time when it flows quicker... More successions of coinciidences... More energy flowin' in and out...And times when we seem to be really moving foreword...Times of recognitions that are very meaningful, vey powerful, and times of empty whatnotment. Mostly the latter.... Tis why I want to kick this old truck into gear...

In the journey of time, with the meaning clues guiding... The love present and nurturing, yet scarcely noticed...and the potential sitting, watching, waiting.... from within... Experiencing life with us... From our perspective ... Hoping for some stuff.... Bored of some stuff.... But always plotting new opportunities for the potential...of it's self becoming realized by us...
Chances for a clue to the whole... Chances for recognition... Chances for life change... Chances for rising in intelligence awareness...finding knowledge...finding some perspective never thought of...finding a surprise, joy, satisfaction...
And lessons!:~]

34.....Go With The Flow

There is a flow to all this... I, through you, have reopened my membership with the arrival team players club...

The potential for an initiation into the soul.

I am also making this up as I go... Which is just fantastic....

And as a self assigned guide roll... I am trying to sincereisize to the max!

So... We are learning to visualize, to listen for soultalk, to recognize the intrepidness of light consciousness, to hold god as with us, to feel our own awareness parameters, and maybe even stretch em', and to reconsider all things!....And to heal.

Heaven, in 3d terms, is simply something you can't see. It's everywhere, though it comes from in us first... But it is a varied flux, an ever interchange of all the varied aspects of space, time, and self.

This "nirvana" of sorts is stupendous indeed, but not necessar-

ily the goal.... Just end phenomena's of natural 3rd dimensional reality... As transcendentalism was never far from normal reality... Normal is maintained by the same people!;)
To me.... It's not attainment, not getting empirical evidence... Not anything other than you have right now!
... Well, maybe a little more, but, to me it is about recognizing we had all we needed all along.... Right in front of our faces!

The truth.

But there is an arrival to the "real" truth...
This is our project with them.

To reach heaven... In 3d... So a transition to heaven of 4d can occur more readily. To expand scope of the big picture.... And to create something anew!

These are basically expanded positive affirmations... And they should be repeated often, because they will fade! They are true though! We can't let something this good fade.... It's not going anywhere.... Were all in this together, for the long haul.... To the end.... Death.
And if it is learned from sufficiently... Rewards!
Not promising anything, though!...
Everyone earns their own... Based on care for as many details, and people as you can, and sacrifice for others.

But... What if realization of truth had its merits...Bet it does....
At the least, it's an interesting monologue...?
Oh well... No room for doubt... I've found that one really has to believe it in order to see it.... It's so darn illusive...

Let's just agree to believe, and go with the flow.•}

35.....Self's Passion

If one can see past self's desire, into self's passion...
We find mass amounts of reverence for.... Most stay at selfish desire motivated...and are never satisfied with their attainments...

and always want more...or the opposite occurs, and they become so content, that no motivation to grow beyond results....
Loose, loose situation ... Where all was in vein... Self has to have passion for attainment for something...but no selfish desire for things of the world.

Could this have anything to do with enlightenment???

Hummmm... Wonder if this is the reason!?

Drop self!

36.....Downward Pulls

Hang tough, buddy!... It's the same for me....

Selfish archetypes won the minds of nearly 70% of earth... Making them limited to self service first! ...and a heavy dependency on ego...Be like the 30% of earth who are like angels...
...Stoic....stoicism transcends all attitudes....
...all the downward pulls

View them as clouds rolling overhead... Can't touch you, unless you tune in to their energy and it saps!

Cloak of insulation is the term for imaginary mental protection shield... To keep out nega nellies!...

We'll work on that!.•}

37.....Don't React

Don't react! Don't get squeezed in the now... Later will come and now will seem distant and superfluous.... Dropping self takes a lifetime!... No quick fix....
Devlin is a joke... Rhetoric
No demon can affect you directly!... The process of not falling

down avenues of frustrate & spent apathy get to me too... Their
long term processes...

Slow down the all right now notion... Now is all were aware of....
But there is much more going on behind our awareness....
Faith in flow ....

...Of time .

38.....Empty Consciousness

Everythingness.. ...It just feels so empty.
Which is the point exactly!
One should continually want to drop notion of "self" altogether

...Indefinitely!:)
I am not is the higher truth, than I AM!:)

...The source isn't all caught up, in needing to be a form...it's cool
with being formless...in fact, it's preferred!

39.....A Way Out

We must figure a way out!
When we feelin' like that about stuff.... that everything sucks...

We need a snap to... Instant out.... That's the going within, with
them , who are already in your infinite field within, who are trying
to give us opportunity , through these.... To get out of any situation
the external world could dish out.
And to be a testament to belief in action!
Ya gotta see how this is harder for me, but I too still need to
awaken... Arrive.... Meet the perfect state... Enlightenment... To go
within...
I'm as normal as day one... I'm the same as you.... Just 10 more
years to word assimilate....
I'm just regurgitating their words... These aren't mine... Mostly
anyway... Some has been speculation and guessing.... But it's in

check with my sources guidelines of logic, and expectation.

Keep in mind, self is many fold... Part of me is arrived already...
The soul.... The subconscious has a pretty good bead on things
too.... but the conscious... dumb as day one... meaning 18 years
old , when I found spirituality, and began philosophy classes, and
theology studies....
I am an empty mind... An ego buyer intoer.... A full of __it, idiot.
Just a guy....

But after 20 years in-light-seeking-ment, American Indians, all religions studies and music.... The esoteric messages from music...
The real gear turners.... The best guides... They put it all together,
and relayed it...
And I'm dittoing....

Can we do something with it?

That's all them and us, are wondering....

Lots of potential!!!!...lots!
Let's work it!!!   We can work it!
It'll work eventually ... .•}

40.....Randomness

Randomization associated freely...to randomize the free associate

Devoid of all thought... vs. ...The never-ending dreamer of count-
less realities....
Both need to be explored... Both are equally important...
The form of all thought gets to be viewed from within!

There is so much we have touched on... Monumental ... Existential.... Finite reality is seeming less and less real.

Did you ever notice reality follows you around?...
Continually at your service?....
Really... Fast and continually....

The upward pull can't break gravity of the individual if resistance to the downward pull isn't put in by the individual.
Most don't want to say no!
They allow themselves to drown.

This can show us something we never expected... Guru potential is closer than one believes... As we are all guides now!

I AM going to go beyond normal parameters of selfhood
I AM an enlightened one....and an anointed one.

When you go to a restaurant, you don't say" gimme whatever"... you tell em' what you want!...tell your order to god's fast food joint... Seriously... They aim to please!

Guide truth! .....Earn vision!

Trusting expectations, faith in abundant energy and love.

The trajectory of our aim determines where we'll end up!...aim high, but not too high!...or it falls back where it came from!

Perseverance is more important than attainment!
Continued refinement of the passion and the vision of unity... And chipping away needlessness... Distortions.... and superfluous-nesses!

Self-betrayal ... Give it up! Along with notions of a self-altogether.

Do you know what to know sufficiently?... At all?.... Or totally?.... or not at all?

Things can change behind our minds awareness...The fix is in.... They, She, & It did it.

Times of toughness can be wiped clean with a little care... Care is always increasable!

I am a promise of potential, from god to me....I am a potential promise to realize god....

Imagine feeling feet on ground ... 3-d reality in front....
Know at this point... Both are illusion....
Truth within…You can sense the limitlessness just behind you!

Self sabotage comes almost naturally!.. Must realize that's the inherent intuition to kill ego... But your real self suffers.. Must stop the contradiction!

How many of us live on auto pilot?... Most to all?... We allow it, by not spotting it!

A trance state envelopes most... It facilitates lies, ignorance, and illusion...like a dream state,,, we can wake out of it!

A higher dream requires a new structure... A new conceptual framework!

The meaning of within....it is being-ness itself!.... Meaning... Were already in… and with!

DNA is Mother Nature... Is your body... Clear light consciousness is your mind... is a feminine creative principle…The light…The source of all, is your awareness… Ever new born! ... The Now, born of me!

Transcending cultural implants..." I'm not ok"... "There's not enough"... "Not likely"...self-inhibitors…that we impose, and can remove!

Spot the illusion... How is it that we feel so separate within all the unity?... How is it that we're blind to the light, but still can see?

Meanings are like vehicles to get us from here to there... But we keep falling out the car!... Use a seat belt, for cryin' out loud.·}

Questioning reality starts the request for council... The guide ship has begun!... Answers are in the midst… discern….
If it feels like a duck…it's probably a duck!

Allowing emotions to express themselves can be a catch .22...cant repress em'…. Can't let em' run free... must find a balance where both are addressed.. as quickly as possible...

Spirit conspires only to give us an opportunity to learn how to reunite...

...Declare your freedom in the power of now!.. Believe it as if it were true!:)...We are all uniquely destined for greatness;)

Lies from our own mind lead to a chronic procrastination...
They tell people what they want to hear....
Fears, reluctance, and doubt stop foreword movement... Unless recognized as a catalysts to doing the opposite!

Commitment to overcome is what it all really comes down to.•)

Failure can seem tragic,... But is there really such a thing as failure, if one learns from.

The houses of anger, fear, and depression are miserably trashed houses.... Who would ever want to hang out in those dwellings?

The moment you give up hope...you declare you don't believe.... Don't need to ever go there.... So much easier to just believe that the light has and always will win over dark.

Imagine 1000 people in an auditorium.... And to view them from within... One sees 2000 holes pointing at the stage.. And all are one eye... No separation of self-conceptualization.... one huge mass of consciousness!

Offering the delicate delicatessen of heartfeltness....
Is required to gain access to the great heart of gold.

I'm not sure if I'm trying to find myself, or loose myself?
Oh...drop conceptual thinking, and become aware of light within... no self involved... just unity in motion on multiple levels simultaneously.

Turn your outlook, to looking into the world, from outside of it, and outside from within, to the world looking in on you, or out from inside you .•}

The heights of godhood are so deep within us that it is nearly un-fathomable.... But it is potential of seed made manifest.... Waiting Indefinitely... Every seed holds all the potential of its source!

The halls of the mind have many doors, and many pictures on the walls.... Wonder what's behind some of the doors?... What pictures are on the walls?... Could they be our own reflections in the mirrors of consciousness?... Into rooms full of mirrors?

An infinity called self is a very big lie...
A self called empty is a lot closer to the truth!
Both are truths, and both are lies.... Based on one's point of view.

This now is instantly becoming nothing more than a picture on a brain cell!....and a copy for the soul's memory....and a copy in your guide's memory,... and a copy for all times memory.

After years and years of accomplishment.... All one really has is now.... All the rest is just images in the memory... And now is so fleeting.. You can't hold on or grab it or stop it.....Forever falling foreword.... Inde-finite Instantaneous flow of now.

Imagine walking around with a gigantic hat on.... I mean big!... Like the size of a house... This is your mind visible.... And we all just walk around with these huge illusions on our heads....Meaning the sphere of awareness we see, is visible as a ball of reality, to them.

41.....Shining Sharpness

Remember... You're merely shaded from the sun in your mind.... And blinded by the clarity of consciousness...

It's ok to just be.
But it's rad to be illuminated!

Funny to me how hard it is to hold on to a train of thought some-times, and others train hopping at high speeds.
Meaning.... We all flux... Different brainwaves...

Sometimes emptiness is all that comes to my mind.... Sometimes-great ideas.... But I don't get too caught up, as there all just dreams.... They come... They go... When we think of time, we think of motion in the outside world... But it happens inside too... We can only hold on to so much, before we have to discard... To make room for anew...

We are so blatantly finite and dreaming, mentally.... Ever changing, ceaseless...and ceasing...incessantly.

None of it really exists... Though it's all of permanent record, and was necessary synapse connecting, and is what we do naturally.

Isn't it almost viewable as menial?...Small potatoes... compared to the potential, we believe to be conspiring with every breath..

...Yes! ...The beyond is so very real, so close to our every thought...

And, so very now...

And pending more consistent, and more depth of recognition, of these transcendental truths, we know by the almighty deduction of logic to be true...

That you are a limitless soul, mind, and spirit...
For real, in shining crystal sharpness...
Always waiting .•}

42.....Thank You

I want to thank you.•}

I don't think I could have done this without you.

You allowed an opportunity for me to blab...and blab I did!

Wow!

I almost can't believe it... Had I not so much damn recognition of everything I know!...

Just that simple...Face to face with the truth, brought to you by the truth, and my minds ability to recognize truth.

Daaaaaamn....G!

Nothing more need be said.

I enlightened myself! ....

...But only thanks to you.... All credit due!

43.....Karmic Accumulates

Well... I realized something about karmic accumulates...

They suck!...energy from us like a vacuum ...mostly forgiveness issues.

Because good karma is mostly neutral... And bad is negative. Each person we had an unresolved issue with has their very own file, in a filing cabinet....We ignore and deny the folders in this particular cabinet most of the time, due to their chronic bringing to mind the negative sap machine they dropped in your head sack.

But they're always there and they can be hard to close, once opened...

Thus should be approached with caution!

Now this is akin to an answering machine everyone will have to check once dead....
And they will have to address each one, eventually.
Nothing ever really goes away, just because time seems to be ceasing and moving foreword away from the "past".

So these files of bad karma... Some from you to others... Some from others to you...All need an old soul referee who knows!...and with a little compassion and forgiveness!

Negative, bad, unfair, power trippers.... all energy sappers.....
Downward pull people.... immature perpetually!... but to have understanding, empathy, and forgiveness... a lesson!

Most are not really bad people.. Mostly just " normal" people, just self-centered.... Aka ... Undecided's... Fool's about simply not playing games with others... So simple to be cool!

So don't try to resolve these issues... Ignore em' and forgive em'... shows maturity and wisdom.... Deal with them on the other side... Where they have nowhere to run!... And must resolve, and confront under the guise of the guide!...

Don't ever get mad at a power tripper again....Just more bad karma energy put into files, who just can't play fair, and don't give a bit about their after life truth preservation accumulate payback!

But they can always just apologize, and never repeat...to let it slide, is always available from the forgiving heart...and most who see their unfairness, usually just walk away from it!

As in the 20/20 hindsight of the after life plane, the after death plane, and the after the 3rd dimension plane...souls just naturally see eye to eye!... Truth is known...Illusion gone.

The truth is one universal agreement!...no duality...just free will to choose ones spiritual orientation, as one see's fit for themselves!

44..... Conceptual vs. Real

The funniest thing about all these concepts about infinity.... Their not seeing it.

At some point one needs to go past conceptual... and become a reality.

A concept is just a mental function ability... Natural ... But real infinity.... Which is inside... and inseparable…

Is not really something you need to seek, find, or attain....

...But maybe to run from!

...Good luck!

That's the big surprise at the end of the tunnel.... Your real infinity... In all its pain, sorrow, angst,... And good stuff... All!

Inescapable....

...Forever... .•)

45.....Forgive Em'

Judge not... Least yea...

Whooddathought... My demise.

Man... Godda let it slide....

Though judgment is true and valid.. If not a civic duty...

Nonetheless... Tis a fault finding grudge match....

And unrecognizing of good stuff... ... Thus fails unity lesson...

Infinity joining... Pending polarization... In symbolville... Here.

End Transmissions...

10/14 to 11/14/2010... one month of an energy-elemental put in, to help a friend...And it worked! ...mostly on me...but still...

Random Thoughts:

Part A:

We are working with the source to get to the goal...clarity, cognitive, and insightfulness...It will get us there, but we must make it happen...With trying, remembering, and reflecting.

The Unity, is mostly an idea, to bring one to compassion and love for others, equally...We share the air, time, awareness fields...All just symbols of a beyond...where we bring closure to the stagnation and illusion of the finite.

The increased frequency of a recognizing of the light in our day to day brings increased mental capacity, and consciousness.

Thoughts based in falsity often self inhibit, ...But the truth always sets one free... Just gotta sift through all the lies!

Most don't ponder theology, due to the conflict...Each declaring a theological supremacy, and a concept of separate, from other theologies....But a source of life recognized as love... knows empathy for life.

Truth Preservation to being Kind....Key to Liberation and Graduation....Naturally, and with out 'trying to do' anything.

Everything in our lives is building up to, and a necessary part of the process, to the next step...which is the great meet n' greet.

In this moment, fall into heart for spirit, the seed of light...In us, around us...is Truth...Clearer than air....everywhere!
We can find it with reason and logic...And become to The Light, and to shine our own!

The lesson of the sludge that binds: can be mistaken for laziness...but based on a vision of a big mental plane within....full of magic, spiritual wonder, unlimited learning....rarely does anyone find it...with all the go, go, go in the outside world...But each day holds the potential to grow awakened, and realized.... I find a pattern of limited, short sighted, self inhibiting, finite "catch up" mind....Never tries to go within, or to expand scope....And yes, the downward pull is to blame too...The culprit in charge wants to keep us in a small finite…it resists exposure to the limitless light consciousness within….I know this light is inside me, because all awareness flows from inside me…from it's source within…who is an infinite source, mind you…DNA intelligence is huge, much bigger than me…The angelic kingdom is really big, and ancient… and is within the infinite….the light is on all dimensional levels at once….We are within the one…all of love…all darkness gets snuffed in the light, the sludge disappears, as it was never really there… just a mind trick of the pull down crew.

Universal love is the concern for others as much as the self…for all life…And a sacrifice for love that is automatic… as it is the root of motive and foundation of intention

A mastery of seeing others for how they really are is no easy feat indeed…realizing what their meaning is saying… their body language… their aura… their unity link to you…. and the coincidental reasons you may have come into acquaintanceship….one can always increase the realizing about other people in your life more!

The old souls… the guides… the angelic intelligence agents do so much more poetic justice than is seen on the surface…more intimate interworking with us in present time than we could ever imagine….worry not!

It's all just an existential switch of perspectives!!!!… The Grand Awakening….occurs in an instant and over a lifetime… but really, one moment of recognition of how things are just beneath the surface…. how things really are… and bam!!!…. You just began the beginning of forever…

Empathy capacity is the gauge for how polarized to the service to others one is….if the drain from the undecided is too heavy…time to regroup, and increase compassion for the world.

Tough love in the form of lessons can be tough to swallow…pride can get in the way of learning….must surrender mental mind struggle… the ego dilution that's clinging on to an old, small, distorted, untruth-preserving mind….and get to following the guide of the flow of time, consciousness and reason and logic.

Part B:

Holographic universe...negative nellies vs. angelic hero's ...recognize the love from above, and there is no duality......no emptiness.

Amongst the sadness, lies, deception, the lower aspects of society and the self.... remember ... there is one who smiles on you... always around.... Always looking out for your infinities' subsequent happy future....

Let your true thought pattern emerge past all negative archetypes... where illuminated comes back into effect... the recognition of divine love flowing from with in us ... thought turns into form... made manifest....the one mind... the law of mind...will work with, and for us... we can trust this.

The soul is certain! ... I should be more certain.... let go of old complaints... old apathies....apply logic to anything and hear its reasons make sense... the celebrated perspective is illuminated.. where you find the beauty in each moment....and can be applied even when not feeling so celebratory..

Words are the end result of a long, thought out conceptualization process....and... the word is the first contact with that concept.... So, one hears a consolidation of meanings, all into one.

Must actually believe the change can occur from finite to limitless!...to reach truths of a real end phenomenal nature... the ultimate truth.... such actual transcendental truths are now clear as a bell... must let go and expect to arrive at the end result... which is now... and here... and expect the with them... and because of them... the elders....in union with the light.... brighter and clearer than the day.

Drop doubt... believe in love.... please....the solution to the situation placed before us here, is up to us... and is with in our capacity.

Trigger mechanisms are in place everywhere to catapult learning... to just sink back into mind... listen and reflect!

Gotta let go of unresolved issues...give em to the seed of universal love to sort it out and fix it...if you forget about it, it will work itself out naturally... especially if you believe!

Stay on the meaning train once you catch it... we always fall off... and forget to finish the realization process... the train will fast track to the other side... if you can hang on!

The nasty negative nellie spirits... vs. the ghosts of hope... no competition really.... acceptance of unity with the ancestral guide of empathy and ethics....is cornerstone to awakening to the now.

Alone is a dead concept... Throw it away!.... Guide is always With.....In!... They are "just like" a best friend.

Communication with the closed minded souls, who are reluctant to try any awakening, should be handled with utmost patience and care!... as they are on a threshold of a two sided fence...and don't wanna push em' to the defense side of things... the shared side is best.

Unity in-place....spiritwise with the molecular universe...old souls and the light of consciousness... result in awareness of the love in-place...

Thinking is merely sub-vocal talk.... inner dialogue... mental conceptual activity... real mind is more intense than riding a surfboard atop a 100-foot wave...

Ignore negativity

I need more reclusion in my life...just beneath the surface of any lie... is the truth ... awaiting! ...Meditate more!

To say a prayer that's so sincere, that it feels like it worked!!
... The call to the elders is always at hand... at your service... how deep is your love?... for others?...the self?... Divinity?... Can you get to the point of sincerity where your willing to give your life for another...that's what they need to know, first...then divine intervention may occur, ...grasshopper;)

Part C:
Source is present...inside and out...does it feel separate or alone?... take it back to the essence!

Who's guiding the reins of the undecided spiritually?.... the judgmental?... the fault finders?... the negative nellies? ... no one's behind the wheel!

The point in mans civilized development where he wrote the first I.O.U.... the first promissory note... was the point where man fell from grace.... the start of all dollars... all greed... and the point where a mans word no longer meant what it said.... or else he wouldn't have had to sign some piece of paper... just live up to your word....Ahhhh... yes, but the convenience of carrying the light weight piece of paper, instead of carrying the chicken across town to go get some apples....

Our sphere of awareness is sharing space with other spheres of more vast scope and intelligence...the older entities awareness field....yet, were only aware of our self... if that!

Source of consciousness will guide you to the top... just let it...if you listen to your sweet self serving song of love for self too long, you'll end up alone, inside.

The Big "Ohhhh"... everyone will get to it eventually...the point where you know... where you realize...and source reveals... the pieces come together...and ...Ohhhh...lot's of little ones along the way... but the big one...just wait!

When in a world of finite minds.... ever forgetting... with pre sorted and pre selected views... with no truth preservations to care for others as much as the self... must apathy rule?.... NO!!! ...Make it infinite, in-light-end-ed.... and truth preserved!.... with the love recognition you earned through care for it, as if it were you on the other side of things.

In the process of coming to serenity of knowledge, completion of lessons, polarization of orientation, and the sparking of the soul.... graduation is guaranteed... but till then... the downward pull from

many people, and within, from doubt and self-focused traps…..
but god present… recognized…shows a smile… so, you get the
picture!

"I'm Here For You"… the mantra of the service to others… this
outlook transcends the self focused, the insecure, the distorted…
you are a valiant and noble intelligence agent from the universe…
here for anyone…to a point… but, selfishness from others does
drain.

Motive is what drives you from behind… intention is what you put
forth….both need to line up with love for the divine, unified.

There is actually no such thing as "Being"… that's a static concept
trick, to fool us… time is ever flowing… faster than the speed of
light and slower than imaginable.. at the same time!

You are real, you are reality… you are also in an element of
conspiracy… so the walls, the floor, roof, air, and your body are
watching your every move… mirroring it… for you!...Every second.

You are a star in your own movie…every second…act like it!... no
second takes… no stunt doubles… just you , the writers, the direc-
tor, and the producers!...And would it kill ya to smile a little more?

Glimpse of freedom…. conspiracy from source unwrapped into an
exhalation of smoke… look at how free we can move in a frozen
finite reality… you can spot the conscious love from above… it is
free will.

Guess what … drop it!.. the whole concept of self as separate all
together…there is aware of others…then aware with others… then
finally, aware as one!... your homies are wit ya at the formless
capacity,,, sorry about the rule of conspiracy….. It's the only way
to have a neutral set and setting.

It's up to me to see past the banter and bickering of the pecking
order people, and remember the one's who's smiling upon me…
…The Guiding Light Source, within.

Part D:

No one ever plans 50,000 years down the road... but guess what... what you do today will be here 50,000 years from now... the permanent memory mechanism isn't just in your head... it's in the head of your spirit guide, as well... their souls have a permanency too!

When something seems hard to get or to understand, it's an illusion for us to figure out, like a maze...but nothings closer to the truth, literally!... there are always many ways to the solution and always the one!... the blindness is weird, I know...but when seen , it's so clear...just see past the vague, darkly of illusion! ... Its only there for administrative reasons.

The pending removal won't leave, till there's nothing left to conceive!

As the theory goes, every hollow soul potential has opportunity to polarize, but if negative propensity carries past half ones life... their 50/50% care for self/others... can't reach the 50/50% mark.... That's what next life's are for, I guess... another opportunity to polarize and spark!... no timeline for those not sure ...eternity will wait!

Silence seems strange, I know... mind you... your "In Time"... Their Not!...it's a test... to drop ego... to build ego... to sacrifice for love... or to sacrifice for no one... or for just a very select few?

You've never gotten one honest moment to just check your life!... to reflect on everything... to realize everything half thought out... the arrow that flies by day is fast... and ceasing faster...the dilution of selfhood...the self as a finite unit of one, without total awareness of anything...because your..."Now Only"

The student is a teacher... visa versa... to not know this... one is neither...

The devil...a scapegoat?...an enemy?... or just a counterpart to wholeness of guidance....aka... impotent... but good for emphasizing the good!...oh, and there is no such thing as... an enemy... A trick word made up by the devil to create duality among brothers

Turns out accumulated karma doesn't go anywhere...permanence of memories is something we don't generally think about...we hide this possibility from ourselves...caverns inside with tons of junk can build up and sneak up in the form of frustration... aka... time squeezed too tight for mind to figure out fast enough...makes one forget about empathy... try to remember.

I think all you need to do is to see today!... the light is ever patiently present and waiting for your acknowledgement.

Socrates spoke of coming out of the cave to see the light of day... but everyone wants to sit in the dark... and chase the shadows the illusionists cast on the wall's...so we think of our minds darkly as the cave... but it's the outside world that's the cave walls... it's in your mind that the light of day to come out of the cave to is... coming out of the cave is actually a metaphor for going within..

Cave mentality vs. jovial child.... the switch... the movement to the "out of the cave" is the part that requires assistance....for it isn't a sneaking in the back door of paradise... it is a process of initiation... with the silence...to learn to listen, and to learn to hear!

To hear the silence for how it really is was the first challenge to attaining visions during meditation...it speaks loudly... just try ... to get into a hearing relationship with silence...A hearing relationship is very intimate... a dialogue with destiny... pride and dignity come into duality with pride and ego... one can keep the first and bypass the second if they hold the vision....we need to drop one and harness the other!

And the hummingbird does fly!...(Seals & Crofts)

Your D.N.A. loves you so much... it is hands down the most taken for granted source of transcendental love we always have near.... the Source is much more subtle... but it's inescapably nothing but love too!...

The formlessness of the Source... and the endless forms of reality are utterly at one.... but one of em' had no beginning!

Part E:
Can you develop a paternistic process to realizing god?

If one thinks along the lines of how can I help others... there is no time for self focus... it just gets taken care of naturally as one is busy helping to figure a way for others to better themselves....

Tomorrow never comes, or dies... it, as a thought, and idea, a dream of potential... for anything... yet there's a continuity of karma .. the pattern... the message from your higher self.. your lesson....till you die...then it's tomorrow.

One must find it in one's heart to understand the reasons for everything, all are based on as much logic as the individual could muster at the time..... to forgive everything.

Faith in flow... spontaneity knows its function... if you allow it, it will resolve any situation... faith in spontaneity is true faith.

All action creates an effect... every thought... every word... is a liability.... that is a permanent expression that can be misunderstood.... we must tread lightly... listen softly, like a lover, to the beauty in every moments meanings.

Going within to a deep meditative state, is like the doldrums of night.... the dead zone, meditatively... the space between late and early... space where cracks in the fabric of reality can occur... where the potential of anything can manifest.

To get mad... ever... is a statement to the unity listening... "I don't care that I'm not alone... I don't care if god's listening... I like negative energy and I dare it to destroy me more".... stop this gambit forever....the contradiction to the recognition of the love of the unity, is uncanny.

I drank the light by reading the wisdoms from the ancients, until I was drunk on illumination.... and a drunkenness from any other source, than the source... is ridiculous!

You are me, and I am you ... one... no separation...and no loss of individuality... it is the false concept of a "you" and a "me", to begin with that is the cause of the dilution.

The cool thing about dealing with the concept of transcendentalism.... is that anything can be anything... make it how you like... and make it up as you go!... but try to hold some preservation of truth, and love.

Redefine: "religious"..."spiritual"..."god"..."angel"..."demon".... reconsider the concepts that lack universal logic for all, and practical use... and the ideas become very helpful and real.... Faith is simply common sense... not religious...reverence for the Divine, and for Life, can be made, simply by recognizing them ...to be within.....and sacred.... lots of socio-religious implants were born into that must be removed, and redefined....Oh,... and Jesus was the coolest guy! ...A genuine hero... and still is.

If love can remain the major premise for long enough durations... it slowly starts to take over to being full time... indestructibly so. Arrival at a full-blown clairvoyant vision of the transcendental reality in place is amazing indeed... but not important to see, actually...just to trust it is there is enough to walk with it harmoniously.

Positive affirmations strengthen beliefs... tis why the theme of repetition... the finite is constantly trying to catch up with the infinite with in... and shouldn't even try... its already in place!...it's your higher self.

When locked in depressed perspectives, angry ones... worried.... one cant see through the negative illusion lock.... no matter how illogical... the negative archetypes of all time are an unfortunate thing to deal with for us lovers of unity...the dude who's job it is to keep you down has a higher intelligence in some regards... and can keep one trapped pretty well, pretty long, and pretty consistently for being the weaker entities!...Till we choose to drop the fear.. the apathy... the frustration.... were letting a negative nellie work side by side with us...just like the first second of doubt... you loose all liberated light power... instantly... and give it to the wrong guy....the devil.

Part F:

The recognition of the permanency of memories is where it all begins... finite, fidgety mind steps into the higher upon recognizing the unseen working with it.

Genuine, sincere, acknowledgement, and recognize are the 4 most important words to me... they are sacred....and I'm working on it! (joke)

Beliefs are solid and unwavering... means no doubt!...beliefs, solidly believed in... everyone will struggle... self doubt.... one is doomed..... if one believes with no doubt... they get the universe handed to them on a silver platter....but to let doubt slip in for even a second, let alone take over....takes away all potential, except to figure a way out of the hole you just dug.

I put my faith in the Source... because it's always sourcing... right in front of my face... like a movie projector...

Let mother nature motivate and inspire you... same with all the rest of the bunch!...old souls, the stuff of souls, and your soul!

Follow the obvious... The right thing to do will tell one what to do... always!

Everyone's room full of darkly funny mirrors is filled with karmic distortions... and supports blocker walls to facilitate ego building...this dilution cuts off the unity and potential for enlightenment completely... a room of self created lies... the emptiness... the ceasingness of time... the countlessness of dreams....the ego... the concept of self separate and alone... and all while knowing that we are not alone... the unseen is so easy to recognize once accepted, and embraced!

Silence may be misinterpreted as empty, nothingness, if not realized to be god it self... listened to like a lover... inspirationally so.

Notion of self is not needed... only a complication and a procrastination to the inevitable end result!... as there will never be a loss of individuality!

Life can seem sometimes to be merely a being used or using others, as all are self's focused on their own to some degree... conceptually thinking they must "be" a "self"??? Whatever that's trying to mean... is erroneous... To live for another vs. to live for the self, back and forth, like tennis... cant be saint service with no self care... cant just patronize... must just resign selfish striving to simply be here more for others than the self... who ever that other is.. a new one can be focused on endlessly!

Injustice causes an ego reflex.... since infancy... that emotion... pissed or dissed... is an auto agreement to pout... instantly in step with negative energy... which is no good... remember ... the negative realm of mental/spiritual energy is a no win situation... ignore it... unfair, injustice is the root of all evil.... they'll all get worked out afterwards... if you know what I mean... everyone see's eye-to-eye then.

Once in a every so while... we catch glimpses of the light... it can spontaneously pop in and interact... one must be ready to recognize it, and follow it... indefinitely...If you can catch the light, and ride it on out...you can enter the unity flow from them, through her, for us.

It's tough to hear the guide... but once spotted... can grow to work with it... and then become a conduit for it... subject/object distinction grows a gulf of doubt... one should expect to go beyond... positive faith with reasonable logical expectations.

The little lie who tried to be true... tried to trick us... into believing its real.... its not... were just stuck.... we choose to shift, constantly.... its love that we're working towards... we must push on through.... recognize the difference between energy sap/drain times... and illuminated/energizing times....and direct our energies accordingly!

The truth is pouring out our eyes... and into our face at the same time.... to recognizes this truth, puts a source of time visualizations in front of ones face!

Unity in place is already ready...all one has to do is believe....

Part G:

If you hurt... don't pray for self... or ask for self to fix self... you can make a deep and profound request for assistance for others... to the service to others angels... and they listen and respond instantly.... but when you call for the self... it's like calling for a service to self....just can't call the service to self...ever!... must believe in yourself, working with the divine... to self heal.. with the higher self, the light, the source, the guide, and your imagination!... just imagine a high tech lazer beam of healing energy beamed on the affected area... soft.. consistently... from with in your deepest height of godhead...imagine light healing energy from within!

Spiritual stability is the key... not attainment of anything... just multi faceted awareness of all that we have, are, have been, are going to be... and are with already!

A down to earth, solid saint service to others stance is the spiritual knowledge and wisdom of the elders... so we may meet them... with a smile.

Insecurities, and self doubts are a big problem, hurdle for people to overcome.... many can front to have overcome... but existentially speaking... we all have them... simply because we don't have confirmation of what we believe and know...listening to others more is one key... to get out of ones own...get perspective from others .... increased knowledge IS power...but you have to educate yourself!

It's easy to ride on auto pilot.... but to be on ones toes... ready for decisiveness....is key to being present with the presence ... for all surrounding others....and what is to come just down the road.

Meanings are energies... can redirect energy by redirecting meanings of things...deeper meanings... more meaningfullnesses... more hearing of where meaning is trying to get us!... It's called perspectivication!

Release, remember, and reach out...remember, recognize and realize...read minds, reap light and reach enlightenment.

Something, unrelated, is very real... as it shines past.

Make the deepening of meaning a practice... as future comes... now builds to epoch... meaning carries on and builds... and point "a" actually gets to point "b".

Give more than you want and your heart will turn the key!

Unity... ego-not-ness... needs to also be sharp and on-point for what is to come... ya never know what may be right around the corner... Spontaneous expansion.

Nothing can block it!... believe it... the change to the unity in place!

The more one realizes their not their higher self... their soul... their entityhood....that it is much higher in awareness and intelligence... the conscious mind doesn't need to know... its known by the soul... and it updates as needed.

Conscious mind is a vital part of the three mind aspects... not inferior at all... not less... just a neutral, empty stage for the now... which needs just that...sure it can seem like a byproduct of the brain, just to do maintenance tasks... but it is the front for the soul to hide behind as well..

The soul is formless and formed.... operating body sometimes.. others just separate... a free multi-taskable force, if you will.

There is a transformation occurring behind the scenes...we know this intuitively... and we know we can trust in it... that it is something wonderful.

You can think... aka talk with the self listening aspect for hours and not know anything you said.... pure finite... now only mind... all vs. nothing... can you believe in the infinity within, deep and long enough?

The coming of the era of universal peace is in process... bring heart and spirit to this transformative time.

Part H:

Enlightenment is coming to everyone... at different levels and gradients... but increased for sure.... bringing us to arrival of many truths... truth supersedes fact... the great spiritual density is pending.

We are pure truth... emissaries of light... let our unified illumines shine.

Light your consciousness ... increase mindfulness of the silence... believe in the empowerment of spirit.

Sometimes I notice that I'm held like a thin piece of paper pasted just on the surface of my eyeballs... with a limitlessness conspiring just behind.... and a perfect lie presented in front of my face... and somewhere in-between is the self, aware of self, ...but where is our source?...our light switch?...out spirit guide?.. we only have an image pasted upon our back lobes....projected from our optic nerve tubes....the perpetual movie theater seat....trapped in it like an electric chair... just never having the switch thrown.

Guides are always guiding... consulting... giving wise advice from eons of experience... and deceptive spirit's are deceiving... equal amounts of insight and deception.... can you discern?

Enlight!... Hold light as a visualization and as a word...light up yourself... don't wait to be lit... or shed light upon you...let it shine... and make it shine brighter!

You are an expression of the cosmos... expressing itself, through you!

if feeling apathetic, or stressed... circumvent a love flow to something admirable... to break the trap's lock's...

Drop old ideas and patterns, stemming from the notions of alone or separate... be open to new perspectives, and visions from the unheard... give the self the comfy posture it deserves, dignified... be here for others, more than they need, or at least as much as you're here for yourself... and make everything in your microcosm magnificent!....Transforming into the transcendental!

Love is the most unused natural resource... and a powerful and valuable one at that!...love isn't about what's in it for me....its rather a tribute to god... others you appreciate... and to the archetypal essence of love itself.

God is flow of eternity....confidence in our invisible partner....free from strain, or doubt...surrender mindless wandering of mind, and study the law of thought.

A golden cord of truth weaves everyone and everything together... the challenge is for us to wake to it.... in recognition, in the now.

When you look into someone's eyes.. can you sense the magnetic fluid?...weather it's positively charged or negatively... and you can see it even though its invisible... look at how different it looks to look into someone's eyes... than the floor, or a lamp.

Presence... is pre-sense...meaning ...before you see it... it's already been here all along!

Anchor your awareness that you are here with god and the co-producer!...whoever that might be???...Your choice!!!

Things are crystalized thought, and thoughts are things...and it's all in your mind!...a big bone to gnaw.

Don't underestimate the soul's potential... the in-light wants to replace the burned out bulbs of the out-lights.

This neverender of time to unfold to the light will always grow... always become one with... will always find truth of... will know all that has ever been known!... in fact, it's already in place!

This self knowing mind... this self aware, and conscious mind is actually totality central!... all spirit, soul, guide, and source... is me... right now...this word is now... and is of me, in now... liberated infinity...in a cute, tiny, symbolic form.

Part I:
Why is it hard for so many to find illumination, when there's so much beauty in every moment?

The illusiveness of recognizing all of these truths and the hardness to remember, has to do with the finite/infinite conspiracy... and the lesson of eggless...and how nice it is to be without egg on your face...and of choosing ones spiritual orientation correctly and wisely,, and not being too lazy to make it real...the more you engulf yourself in recognition of the source vision, the light vision, the spirit guide vision, and the vision of our own D.N.A. being much more than we thought.... the more recognition comes naturally.

Move from insecure about god as a presence of love... to confidence... move from fear based, and apprehensive.... to purposeful decisiveness!

If there were an unresolved issue about the duality/ intrinsic necessity of man and women...I would like to give my two cents take...The Source of life puts its sources of life higher on a pecking order than the protector of that life... they are more mature, more aware, more intuitive, more in touch with the light, than men... as a base archetype... yet as new souls, have the same lesson requirements as guys.... so equality ... AND a perch to be worshiped, should be the stance... as the source of your best friends life, deserves that.... basically gals are like humble gods... because they don't really know their goddesses, yet... thank god....:)

We build up a wall for years to give a sense of security, isolation, separation... and it can come down in an instant... just one moment is all it takes for an ever waiting light to pour in...but really its already poured in... its just invisible light.

Maximum strength metaphysics... dream beyond... be an outlet... listen deeply.... empower with blessings and admiration...all things work for higher reasons... if love is the first premise... then the result will be the same... and we will bring the unity in place.... In the Place!

Where the concept of oneness and the reality of it lie undefined to us... there is a clear and concise threshold where consciousness meets the spark... the epiphanical moment...Bam!

We are always and perpetually becoming one with the source light...something were always with... and always awakening to... forever... it is as simple as the natural unfoldment of time occurring right before our faces...any time we wanna check it!...the spontaneous clear now of eternity!

The divine mind and transcendental forces are bringing in the new era.... transforming everything...just a little bit at a time... so it's unrecognizable.... It's mostly just a continuing and enhancement of the shared mental unity that's always been in place at the molecular level.

It seems, in retroflection...love is a balancing...a remembrance... a recognition... a belief... a faith... a hope,... a promise... it is eternal... so rest in that!

The final realization... I am a divine being... for real!...oneness... unity wants to reveal... tries constantly... but we resist... the ego wants to cling... control... make a private self encapsulated sanatorium...let go.

Divine unity of all living souls induces a profound love... deeper than anyone can imagine... a passion for the divinity of love... for the love of god... source union.

By me...to me... through me... as me... the process of man to god and back to fellow men...with no illusion or delusion of alone or separate....inspirationally speaking... not me, specifically!

To god: ... you are me... all I see... I thankfully surrender to all your flows... word G!

Someday we'll realize all this... and that we put it on hold for no real reason... except laziness, disbelief, procrastination, doubt, reluctance... but it waited always... conspiring for us to have a neutral stage... all our health and mind came from it all along.

Part J:

God lives in us... breaths in us... we must recognize it... we must surrender to it... for love, respect and reverence...sacrifice to love ... for love... become one ever so more with the essence of love...

If there is one thing wrong... it's called ego tripping... peers compete way too much... we compare each other to each other, when we are all unique set of circumstances, that justify and explain all our results.... there becomes a lacking of the remembrance of love... disdain results... we hold grudges against our peers/lovers for way too long... with way too much negative energy...... it must be ignored... forgave... or released to the universe to sort out....we can find a way to put positive spin on any negative thing...we just need proper dignity in place...then mature stances follow.

People who have a comfy cocoon of self separate sufficiency... haven't embraced the unity vision.... don't know about the viciousness the unity with people who really don't care is like... if they knew... they would focus on love more and more than you would think is needed or normal.

Divine love and the source therein are providing and infusing us with vital life force energy... the base fundamental essence of existence...recognition of this truth can induce joyous consciousness called oneness with pure core energy!

Negative nellies are here to find their like minded... they care not for love... or good... or ethics or empathy...they want their "poorly thought out souls... the selfish bastards... the criminals... and the angels... they want us, the beings of love, to prove it with empirical evidence... and a solid and unwavering consistency of thought and action in the direction of helping others.... ever notice a large percentage of the populace is not at either of these two extreme levels of selfishness or selflessness?

To love the self as much as others... reverence for all life... is to meet truth of the guide....and the super elders.

An energy field of love is generated by love light... which is fueled by gratitude...the key to attaining profound illumination...recognition of the love in place... the love from above... always pouring down... up from below... within... our cortex.... is a key recognition point.

A spiritual practice is required to connect with the limitless potential within...meditation, dancing, stretching, praying, chanting, singing, hiking, volunteering ...and there are a lot more routes.

The word love becomes the key to accessing the unity awareness.... it is the end result of a long thought process that had to choose and sacrifice in order to end up at the end result...universal love is the choice of wisdom...If ones whole of focus becomes more continuous in recognition... acknowledgement...gratitude... and the giving back of love... the multi levels of love ... as one lump sum... will manifest new love... all based on how much one recognizes the love coming as a love found!

To stay on this meaning train eventually will arrive at a junction where truth meets ultimate truth...if put as main meditative focus... bringing this realization to a focus point... and there we can hold it.. to see and to grasp... the light.

Believe the end result is already in place, and you'll get there faster!

Time, consciousness, and the flows of the two.... are a constant puzzle right in front of your face... moments are moving from one to the next seamlessly... with no real recognition ability possible....just the amazement that it really is like magic....and the fact time can be viewed as pouring out ones eyes... or pouring in... or both at the same time... this flow can be imagined as faster than the speed of light....or it can be real mellow like a river...we can choose and adjust it!

What happens to the love vision of illumination?... do we forget?... did we not really have it in the first place?...cant we see how important it is?... how real?... how sacred?... hold the vision... make lit, the light within.. and expect to walk into the infinite mind.

Part K:

Souls that polarize to the negative side... the dark side... the selfish side... the careless for anyone ever side...are a sad study... because they were tricked into believing it was something to believe in... it is a trap ...as, in the unity... a declaration of self only! Get's stopped at self!... it can't go past the self...impotent master of selfish motive ... never to share the unity... which is much... much bigger... and more powerful!... talk about self imposed limitations!... next level of that.

Superficiality takes a lazy route.... so shallow... so insincere... so flakey... basically non existent... yet patronizing ....the mantra of "I love as long as there's something in it for me"... is the problem... the childish stance... not recognized as immature, due to the blinding power of pride....ego wins again!

Remember that All Love is sourced from the divine... weather from in you, or to you... give credit to the sacredness... the divinity in the molecular universe... we are it... it is here!

The stillness is a blessing, and a lesson... it is sacred... and it is a lie... it hangs out with silence because they go so well together.. they love you ... they are always with you... waiting for you... to inure in to the silence, and the static,, and become one with what your already at one with... the light...in cloaked form.

Consistency is the key... truth preservation... genuineness... sincerity... no matter how much it bends,.. the heart wont... a positive expectation of want is good ... want is not all selfish... but the service to others concerns for others as much as the self... and the want will help others anyway... wants can become needs...its truth to need love... one must also, give and show it consistently.

Thought process stops flow of light visions.... stop thinking when in recognition of the light...

One can never be grateful too much... ever increasing.

To move forward in god realization, we find that it is god revealing through mysterious ways, that make it seem like we did it all on our own... but it was it flowing through us... unrecognizably ... yet clear as day... consistent enlightenment cant stop....it is the flow...one of the many in the now... (time, consciousness, guide)

Don't let t the small things that can pull down ever do that... they never have enough heart to give em' the time of day...remember ... the intrepidness of divinity lay silent... rule of conspiracy... hold the light as a sacred concept... to becoming a sacred reality.

The miner's hats... with the light... those are as close of a symbol to the real thing as one can get... the light guides through the dark... were in the dark right now... and the light is visible!

Acknowledgement of the guides around us is important... thank your guides once in a while...if you can do that , you are a wise man...(smiling)

Self apathy and doubt are the point where we give up our power to know in serenity with clarity...the point where we let in the negative archetypes... and go inferior from illumined... must stop the self loathing the sad song of a self called nonexistence...But there's always potential waiting to be real-eyezed!

The conspiracy of spirit is all or nothing... hang in there... it does inch forward each day... each time we try... to remember.

Mental conceptuality is silly ... when it's heard by many... it's like you just want to hold on as long as you can... to the notion of separate and alone... when you see there is no distinction between subject and object... you'll see how silly thought process really are. (rhetoric)

Not being ... but, just allowing... is the definition of liberated... the clothes and air outside your skin is a unified molecular field... the stuff inside you are a unified molecular world,... and there is no separation between the two worlds... unified continuity in the one molecular universe... everything is utterly at one!...I know... skin seems alone... and an effective separation conception tool.

Destiny is active, fluxing, and kinder than is recognized...when seen from the 20/20 hindsight perspective...of the after side.

Part L:

A vision about getting all of us in a unity awareness…a total awareness of all in one… one in all… is true, existentially…in fact its already …in place… but the illusion of static separate… results in what you see… they are the core problem with everything… they root and stem all dilution, and distortion…trying to fool us… but we can spot it!

Why does my ego reject believing in itself when put face to face with the light?….. the ego is tricky… because it's the core monad of entity-hood…and a clueless earthling….the god-head of eternal access to the unlimited reaches of all the soul is now, the brain is now, and the mind is now… and when shared with all living beings, and the vast data bases they share…become available to the seeker …and it is then the falsity of the short sightedness of ego that stopped it's guiding wisdom ….that we are with the ancient wisdom of the guides.

Must discern distorted consciousness and relink the transformative consciousness that is the new now! …pending recognition…. just like the clear light of reality… just like the genetic intelligence consciousness… just like the source of time in motion…like all the love it took just to give you this precious, simple, fleeting moment.

Never give up hope in an arrival to becoming the higher self/soul, …and arrival to the angel's unity, alike.

The negative spiritual downward pull on a very service minded person can only go so far… there's too much love for others to drown in self delusion….and not enough potency in the immaturity ,of the gorilla warfare tactic they use…It's funny, in fact…The negative spirit pecking order leader no longer expends resources on the kind soul…It's the people around you in the world that aren't quite as realized…..And the service to self entity starts revealing it self through others who haven't decided to give equality to all souls…and unity …and are still clinging to the notion of ego-hood… alone and separate…and a strive for self….and an attitude like what's in it for me…to help strangers… and to realize time is fleeting, and that the only thing that really matters, is to keep the continuity of love karma preserved…

Preconceived, misconceived notions that are conceptually con-ceived are missing the point.....one must stop judging others from their own room of mirrored self reflection... and listen to how oth-ers are with an open mind, and a compassionate heart... putting empathy first!

Self meditation is always dreamlike... very deep senses... but the potential for anything!... to go beyond... to have an experience.. to be moved...to change...Just expect it!...and to meditate with another increases awareness field double!....And if the two can come to the hardest thing to do...the legendary eye to eye facing meditation.....Is the most proof in anyone's face that we can see the light in another's eyes....intense, to say the least.

Most are stuck in a mythic/ tribe mentality...unfathomable light is super meta-physical.

Everyone will receive poetic justice upon death!...positive or nega-tive...It will be sweet poetry in motion either way!

Trapped in negative perspectives needs to get out quick!...assign blame to negativity itself...make fun of it's deceptiveness... and get back to the empathy!.... show you can transcend the attitude trap...as nothing is solid or fixed, unless we make it so.

No motivation to do anything?....It's tellin' ya...time to go within!... just ask the monk who's been meditating in a cave for 20 years... How to occupy time enjoyably and intrepidly?...Drop out!... Come inside to the universal mind....The magic stage...sorry your personal infinity has to hide all the fun... but you haven't dropped your illusion of alone, yet.

We can hide stress with denial, but it must be adjusted to at some point...or else the soul can get too bogged down, and want out!... And inhibit healthy living...Balance is key!... Repressing stress simply puts it on hold....But expressing it brings negative energy in the house....the proper perspective always transcends! ....Finding it is the challenge...But not an impossible one!

Part M:
A note on what I think happens when we die... this is meant to be a celebration time of graduation to the next level... if we believe we are gonna remain after, with our truth preservation record... and we finally meet the elders ...otherwise, we simply cease to exist... I bet we remain... due to the meaningfulness of meaningful memories in our lives...the responsibility for all our actions we must/should account for... and the fact, all the reports from enlightened books,... keep saying it's a really cool place...older and bigger than us.

No need to fret or worry about loved ones staying in contact forever!...instant access to them is always within!...It's an age old process...nothing new...even if it entails getting judged... or not graduating...with eternity, there's no timeline... and with a source of love... there's always another chance.....just my take...

The source is planning on a new thing, where divinity begins to reveal itself, through us as vessels to and of it... we are going to change... if we stay open to it... seek steadfastly... and listen like a lover.

Alternate title thoughts:
Source Recognition: Seeing Past The Illusions of Unconnected and Apart, And Obtaining Knowledge From The Formless.

Universal Love: Finding The Presence of The Light and Old Souls Within, And Discovering Boundless Admiration Therein.

The Universal Mind: Determining Everyone's A Limitless Soul, And Finding A Way To Know This.

The Clear Light: Dropping The Delusion of Selfhood, And Becoming One With What Your Already At One With.

Enlightenment Manifest: Turning Beliefs Into Imaginary Realities, And Listening For Higher Truths.

God Realization: Finding Eternity Hidden Within Us, And Making It Real.

All pessimism and apathy contradicts gods belief in me... can't I at least just believe in myself, half as much as she does?

Super old souls like Jesus, Siddhartha, and Gandhi: Bosses to our spirit guides, and the administrative body that makes all decisions for the universe....Sorry about it's dictatorship, but Love is the Law.

Spirit Guide is the super subtle pure love and wisdom of "letting it be"....truth's work their magic ...eventually...inevitably...

Faith and confidence that the new initiate to mind, will find the mind.... and how to drop the distortion conspiracy, the ego struggle, and the negative archetypes....Recognize the light of source within, naturally!...Then proper justice due, may unfold... but till then...the cloud chamber of illusion can bog ones life for decades... and only till one spots it... then it stops!

I spent my whole life being nobody... trying to fit in... trying to be somebody...to no avail...Till I realized to stop trying to "be" anything... let alone "somebody"....and to let myself be empty...and make empty, my self concept....ever dissipating, till one can see their not alone.....but rather a power house within a legion of ancient super heroes....

As eternal souls... all time in 3rd is looked equally, as just time in 3rd... forget it... once in 4th, everyone shares the one!... forever hence forth!...And all that is required,... is to simply have equal compassion, and empathy for the least of us, as much as the greatest of us!

Most people have inconsistencies of truth, of how they are towards others, in regards to themselves, in general...whatever serves em' at the time!...Flip floppers!...always tell ya what ya wanna hear....in hopes for selfish gain of some kind....but they always seemed so service to others before!...till they showed their true colors.

This is a biography of a bid for enlightenment...an on going work in progress....pending acceptance or rejection....upon death.... either ways cool.

Part N:

I guess I put together a circle of truth...it's the philosophers goal...
it works for me...I feel I am a good conveyer of my most valued
concepts...though I don't claim to know the light, god, spirit guide,
or DNA...I do sense them imaginarily...and believe in em' devout-
ly... So, I feel I can reiterate the many truth consistencies from the
many books I have searched out and read.

We generally trust our perceptions...they are mostly spot on... I
always trust em', unconditionally!...But every once in a while one
can misperceive...this is a distortion revealing a lesson...when
we must bow our head... admit shortsightedness.. ask for forgiveness... and move on!....To personally address the lesson revealed
and figure it out is hard...but it should be tried, none the less...It
shows em' we know we don't know all there is.... at all...But if we
think otherwise... we fall.

The subtleness of the downward pull is so deceptive...it's heat
gun work's on us on multiple levels... from stuff in denial on the
unconscious, from distortions, set up like bowling pins, to feel
squeezed in the subconscious...we are gonna be challenged,
tested, and taught!....One way or another... the pull need's to be
spotted by everyone...and can be stopped by everyone, as well...
So....The less love is remembered....more negative energy has
potential to sneak in....and make our time negatively influenced...
it's a win for them...but to shoot one self in the foot...by imposing
judgment, instead of admiration flows,.... blame games, scape-
goats, instead of accepting responsibility, even if none is due....
making others a problem, rather than finding a solution to the unity
....one can drop through the ice by their own doings, be all wet,
very cold feeling, and missing a foot, as it is truly missing the point
of doing onto others as wished back... the good karma golden rule
of fairness for all!

Most won't ever see enlightenment texts from thousands of years
ago... nor the amazing modern works that have the hallmarks of
being truly enlightened...So, I hope to bring all my simplest assim-
ilations to the general reader that they would not have seen otherwise....Visions and thoughts... making connections from "The
Source"..."The Light"..."The Spirit Guide/Angel"...These concepts
are realizable simply with.... thought, belief, and recognition!

Imagine a room is being shared by many... and the set is assumed to be for us, in the room...no one else but us here, right?...Well, Source Time, and D.N.A. Intelligence are here, just silent... we think the room we share is actually out there, out in front of us...but it's not!... it's flowing out there from inside all our heads simultaneously, and we merely agree to meet, at an arms length away... in the room...but really we're all inside each others heads...as reality is inside us, first!

Angels don't have ego's anymore.... demons still do!...building up for lifetimes...in 3rd and 4th...only to be stopped at 4th... no 5th possible for demons!...A dimension of light ,with no separation possible...stopped in their tracks!

I perceive that my soul is busy working with other souls of my friends, other souls of a higher dimension, working with the souls of deceased relatives...lot's of work with lots of other souls... constantly... not enough time, even when out of time!

Many in 3rd are set for graduation to 4th...many pending polarization of orientation lesson/decision still.... and the graduates set are under strict scrutiny...The others can dream as long as they wish... no big deal... any given life holds all there is to life....just like this one.....each just a passing opportunity... a potential to be kind, or be selfish.

Time can be viewed as molecular decay... a piece of furniture from 100 years ago is decayed 100 years worth ...at woods decay rate...in science, we gauge time by the number of electrons emitted by a piece of rock with decay...but quantum physics proves that nothing is provable to exist... as the electrons move too fast to measure... we can only take a picture at a time... but cant track the electrons from one frame to the next...no matter how fast the film technology,....time is faster than light.... Much faster!...immeasurably so....means unfathomably so!

Some souls in 3rd have unlimited access yet are still selfish?...To use the unity for selfish gain?....man, where's the logic?

Part O:

I would also like to mention the vast amount of empty space in every molecule...The neutron and the however many electrons are like a few granules of sand for the electrons, and a piece of gravel for the neutron....These small things are to the atom they are within, as the grains of sand would be to the Island of Iceland.... vast, vast amounts of empty space! And a side note: If an apple were to be the size of earth... it's atoms would be the size of a grape....and in each grape.... 99.9% empty space!!!!

Hang tough!.... There is a presence working with us!....God... Source, whatever ya wanna call it...The sum total of all intelligence inherent in existence.....base provider of base existence requirements....is in the house! ...Subtle, never blatant, just constant truth preservation of the truth...of it's presence, for us, it's joy, for it's beloved mystical consciousness units....called souls!...It doesn't mind you taking it for granted ...indefinitely.... forgetting about it...doubting it... it loves you unconditionally ... forever,....,,mostly because it doesn't have to parent us....per se'....In that case, it would probably get driven nuts!... Nonetheless, god is near!...just faster than light.

The hardest thing for man to comprehend is how everything is blended and it's not black and white...the limitless gray area... can even bend perception to see good as bad... hence, the need for much discernment! ...Not ever is anything "Either, or Or"... but rather "Both, and And" .... Is the case with most things, yet we only see one side at first, and leave it at that....the multi view is tough, but all perspectives are equally valid.

You can't conceive something that's not gonna be there anymore!:)....(ego)

People can mistake this 3-d world for real existence....but the finite shrinks... it does not exist!...it simply goes bye, bye!...The seemingly static-ness of the world, vs. the disappearing act time put's on...can seem permanent ...but should be seen as it is... temporary only!

The light is so separate from selfish people/souls....It let's em' think they got it's backing, and pulls the rug after death.... To build a sense of success...So the lesson sinks in deeper....not to send anyone to hell... ever... souls only go there by choice... the philosophy of self only... The negative uses the light to trick, but no one can blame the light...only themselves.

About having to use Devlin to teach lessons, tough love hurts pride, and ego...but aren't they false anyway...let go of the illusion of alone, and there's no self to be considered separate.... nothing for Dev. to sap fro....But if he does get under yer skin, and ya feel trapped in anger, depression, or fear....just let it pass...go within to the silence of the flow, and escape!

If you were to hear god say, "Sorry about all the confusion, mystery, and tragedy in life"....Wouldn't it make it all less frustrating, less worrisome, less depressing?... Guess what....They sincerely apologize... they understand how tough life can get... it's just the only way to have neutrality... even stage... no favoritism.

I guess you gotta go through some distortion to find clarity.... to get to a low point in life... where there's nothing left but up... as you been down so long, you know where that's going...nowhere....but enter, god...the most high, present...and we finally see the end in sight...in the end we always find the light.

Service to others minds share... selfish ones don't... Ironic... that's exactly what everyone's gonna get when they die....so they say...Those who care for others get care from the divine... those who don't share... don't get to share the one....but they don't have to go to the service to self souls, pecking order place, by any means....just another round here....no big deal! ...but still...why delay?

Empathy can get drained...but it shouldn't be able to... to be true empathy...it's unconditional!...let the drain be your gauge for how well your polarizing!...less drain, means more solid to being service minded!

Part P:

It heals, sustains, and sets us free!...Increasing our awareness of the presence is hard ... and lot's of emptiness...vast amounts, in fact!...Everyone's like "what can I do?"....Just know at this point... You Are Known! You can realize what this means, and that it is an ever expanding realization that never ends...surrender our shadow world, where we're diluted to think were alone and separate.... from god and the meta energies...remember... if you feel tired... it's the opposite sapping...Because it's about what I can do for god... not the opposite...remove self and you're a vessel....There are walls , structures the ego/self put up for a desire for aloneness...But what if there simply transparent?....and the sanctuary we thought we had... where no one could know us....was totally exposed!....What's the point to holding them up anymore?....There is no point....They're utterly seen through by unity people...within and around...Let go of imaginary walls of fear....Shadow times can make apathy, self pity, and depression energy overwhelm... take note... that's not illuminated...in joy recognition of source unity presence...makes god scratch it's head, and say, "Why so sad?"...and you can't come up with an answer worth complaining to god about...you simply got boondoggled by the shadow people...negative nelly wins again!...We were made of love, and love is the sustaining of the vital life force energy...pure life essence...within... the source of all life...brought to you by your own consciousness...

Self is of Divine love... always... seeing this is hard...but should be easy as pie...your etheric intelligence agent is always giving sensible advice.

Two realities exist...one we see...and the one where we don't see the long term effect of our actions...the domino chain can be seen by the guide... as to where one is tipping the balance.

All ego bashing aside... the poor word, ego, is abused... as a bad thing...but it's simply just a concept, or a notion of selfhood...not actual selfhood... which is infinite...just the one trapped in time... The trick is to simply move past being an empty concept with no consistent logic to back it....to one filled with love light!

I would like to clear up any wonder about horror movies... and the negative energy they purport...their all distorted!...Can never happen...not because there is no evil in the universe, in the world, ...But because of the rules in place, to give us a neutral set and setting here on earth... we won't be getting taken over by negative spirits, or whatever....if there were no angels keeping things in checks and balances as good as they are... things would be worse.... The super old souls keep demons at bay....the elders.... the beings of light....the referee...No war up there!... just law and order of the policies of doing onto as wished back!

I have read so much on meditation, chakras, reports of the unexplained, on enlightenment from many different religions....as a theologian, I look for the consistencies, and don't focus on the differences, yet I do listen...And I believe there is validity to each... and when put together, show a very big and weird conspiracy going on from god... bigger than any man could concoct....Right in our own heads/minds...God is silent...aware of us from within... and from without...The energy and intelligence to every cell... Brains are fantastic cloakers of certain truths...but the truth of itself ...is clear as day...right in front of our faces....silently at your service!

Realization of all we know is hardly addressed... but it's all pending....always!.. The art of realization is a hard feat....but possible!......I found that making notes...and putting all the written down notes into my head all at once, like this book, can bring all to recognition... and thus pass whatever test time can throw me.... Same with god realization...finding the light...hearing the guide...and knowing the soul.... tests that need study, and when all perspectives are in recognition at once... one can see multiple levels of reality simultaneously!....That is the goal of this.

Note on arriving.... most want to just wait for it to be handed over naturally....by doing nothing....as a surprise to slide in one day..... and it can do that,...and some say one should simply sit back and wait for the light to rise to being recognizable...others try to find with all their might... and still others just have faith...all are ok!... no either or... but rather a both, and a whole lot more ways to get to the same spot!... the source.

Part Q:

Traditionally it is through a dedicated practice done religiously, with a passion for the divine that transcends all selfish motive... A dedication to thinking, connecting the dots, and accessing the infinite...A sacrifice of self wants for a greater good....and a unquenchable thirst for knowledge, and to find the truth of the source of time.

When addressing patternistic problems....addictions that are bringing us down....I would like to give my take...Eating, sleeping, shopping, talking on the phone, even thinking too much, can be an addiction... and we do these because it feels good.... But they can destroy us....real addictions, that I don't even want to list,... can be overcame with logic... that we don't need it, can learn to be fine without it, as it is hurting our lives in some way...When I had to quit a daily pattern for health reasons, I was finally faced with applying that logic I always had about the pattern...smoking is not good to breath...says it on the label...yet after years of trying to quit....finally, I did!... I think I was helped by the unseen crew... Because the downward pull will get hot and heavy, wants us to get short sighted, and fall into traps....We need to quest to attain the within... not things of the outside...that harm our lives....logic will make a path...
It's up to us to take that first step.

Stoicism is key!...Nothings ever as it seems...nothing as bad as it seems at first, ...not as good either,...the nothingness is ever unfolding to reveal the unseen, the perspectives not seen before, the truth!

Beautification of intelligence occurs with wise decision-making... unwise decisions result in stupidity...But if learned from, and not repeated...a humble wisdom replaces the shortsightedness.... The level of care in our decisions actually results in a pattern towards wisdom... or towards ignorance.

The guide of spirit, the angelic guardian who doesn't parent, the etheric world intelligence, the service to others old soul, the one who's invisible to us, but not to themselves...On the soul plane.... is present.

Most think a god of judgment is something to fear or ignore... when neither is seeing this for how it really is...It is awesome that there actually is someone who can come to a definitive conclusion about everything!....And everyone always forgets about the love...all the love in our health, our intelligence ...from god....that love stays in truth preservation!...Forever!

Guidance is never black and white... in fact, the learning from mistakes keeps one at their continuity of lessons... If ones motive is love based... things tend to find a way to work out ...discernment, intuition, feeling sensitivities... There are always tradeoffs to any decision, and perspectives we won't be able to see till down the road... You, The Guide, and Time... The great equation... They know how you want it to turn out... they do too!... together with them, we can get there.

Must unlearn fears to find love everywhere... The divine loves us like parents... but no parenting... Love will always find a way... send love to em' all... positive or negative people... Love is watching you... to see if your care levels are in check... Automatic love for others... is egoless.

The grand test of faith... Love... For when one can control their love capacity for others, and life in general... and make it how it ought... Then the light is finally on! ... Now, destiny can twist fate, and mountains can move!

Apathy, Frustration, and Fears are the lack of recognition of love... all joy potential gets lost... A great soul would find confidence, and wit, to create something spontaneously cool, in times of being tested.

This life is two things to me... 1- just a short time on a long journey... 2- It is all there is, all I need, and holds all that can be pending... So one must be two fold... Stoicism... go with the flow... hold on tight, but not too tight... And at the same time... realize, This is It!... The one chance you've been waiting for... your right now... your potential... your life!

Part R:

They say there is something inside... a love... That is beyond words... For one to find love, sought after in the world, is awesome... but to find the rumored, hidden one inside... is the greatest love, they say.

I hold all the attributes of a Deity... eventually... divinity in place can spark and become your unfathomed future self!

To truly find illumination... put's one in step with dreams becoming a reality... Not selfish to seek, if one dedicates to the service to others attainment of awakening to the love within!

"The finite mind" is saying...there has to be more!..."stop believing in the objective world" is saying... it's not separate from you... comes from within you!... "We and our source are in unity"... is saying keep an open mind... something might be right around the corner!

The most inspiring thing I have ever encountered, is to be told by someone else, that they believe in me! ... As we all have a challenge to believe in ourselves more... or more righteously, so... And the biggest problem with believing in oneself, is that it feels service to self-like... Mainly because we don't know the soul well enough to identify with it... and we know intuitively that we don't want to believe in our ego, existentially... But when your doing it for someone else... Believing in yourself... nothing can stop you... Because you want to impress and prove true, the one who believes in you!

Lacks in confidence, momentary intolerance to stuff, pessimism... all stop the recognition of the gifts of time... always coming... cloaked, hidden, and unrecognizable... but always with the hallmark of love from above... Just tread lightly... all things pass... all fears are silly... all frustration is short sighted... and all apathy is ungrateful... Must just balance with the hesitation to truly believe in oneself... and just find something to be grateful for, and flow admiration in that direction... to circumvent the flow of focus on self.

Once one says, "This sucks"... or "I'm Bored"... one makes it so! ... To occupy mind enjoyably, intrepidly, and naturally ... without external world stuff... One needs to drop face value of life... try to go within... to the universal mind... the magic of the anything, finally able to be anything... Your personal conspiracy from god is hiding all the fun... the unity... can make one feel empty, cut off from anything other than the now... But it's not ever, forever!... the reveal comes, eventually!

Death is natural, ancient, and inevitable at some point in everyone's life... needed... It is graduation to the next level... Transcendental awareness... reunited with the soul, loved ones of past, and the guide... Emancipated, liberated, redeeming good karma chips... acknowledged for all one has done!... Unsung hero's get just due, finally... And everyone can join the shared unity of the elders.
Point being... worry not... it's age old, and carefully watched for.

So, as a soul, a body, and a mind... all being like a vessel.. a container...and also a vehicle... in that containment unit of motion... we are either alone inside, or with the divine... As a dropped ego... notion of separate self.... we still are here... so we then assume an identity of spirit centered, no longer self centered... and as a part of a greater spiritual unity... we share, we contribute, and we help... as a vessel to the loving nature of the source of light, within.... Always waited within and for each and every one of us!... And forever more, too!

To completely block out negative vibes of the many forms, is a lesson... because the natural reaction is to fight fire with fire, to call out others in the wrong... or to submit to the duality... all are wrong routes... the wise, mature and loving stance... is to stay chill!... Don't go there!... any form of negativity is evil.... we can fill our world with 100% positive light!

Must slow down once in a while to notice time and mind flows as a revealing... an unfoldment... a becoming to... a balance between self focus, and listening to another... or better yet, both at the same time!

Part S:

As we further into god realization, as a presence, we see it's like a mellow river raft ride down a stream... god's river of life...time... bringing a new view every couple of minutes... a journey... an adventure...where we are no longer walking alone on land... the motion of the flow of the river is transcendent to the static-ness of the land next to the river... Now in flow of motion... spirit and time... if you can see it as an unfolding... each moment is an enlightenment...all that is needed is watchfulness, to observe, learn, and steer around obstacles... All rivers meet the see... and god is the river/time/flow that carries us with it...to the unknown, and back to its source....otherwise time will seem to repeat the same moment over and over every minute of everyday.

This vessel we become, not only brings god to the world through us... but also brings us back to god... We are all in conscious cooperation with the divine all the time... just silently... The total of mind and thought that we circulate, are the factors that manifest the potential of the invisible to become visible... In a metasuper moment... We can recognize we're surrounded by compassion... and that we are one with it... and that it is forever.

To be a vessel to the divine, in theory, one must be able to change... to move from old patterns, and maintain an open mind... a change for good, for self, and for the surrounding world, is the goal... The problem is that we keep asking creation to recreate our limitations each day, simply by not spotting how illogical, and limiting they are... Stay centered, open to healing, and a new view... a bigger picture... push past familiar awareness within, and the repetitiousness of the objective world... to find the truth of light within... if only conceptually, we will move in that direction accordingly... and any challenge only strengthens our vessel... as it merely refines our resolve!

To Recognize Them... The Guides, The demons, The Referees... The Elders of Light... of the antiquity of all time...makes one no longer merely a self, king of a sense of separate and alone... To adjust notions of selfhood to one of connected and for purposeful reason... You are the new self concept!... Simply by recognizing them!

113

Revitalizing Love: To end on a practical note of love and unity...

I see so many lacking a reverence for love, to the one their with, I had to give my most sincere two cents... but I know no one needs to be told how or why to learn how to sacrifice for love, but it might help someone...

1st is to remember "All The Love"...all the good times... the smiling eyes...the passion of the beginning...as very meaningful.

2nd is to realize most are trapped in a distorted pattern... that contradicts love....and the fact it keeps repeating, is saying that something is not getting resolved, just found a way to look around it, again... but still feeling something's amiss...for in the beginning it was never there... frustrated and squeezed moments in time... results in communication breakdowns, and unskilled debates. And the reasons for the breakdowns....the understandings of the why, is easy in 20/20 hindsight...make-up's can occur... but the theme of repetition seems to reemerge, and with increased intensity, and both must agree to stop, in the name of the light present!

3rd is to get back to the love... as we all want... because we've been building into it for a long time...and a lot of very special meanings are held with in... and your the same like minds, a divine match, a rare catch, and lucky to have each other. So forgive all the shortsightedness, the bad reactions, the false distortions, the heartless moments, the unmeant words, the power struggle.... all the negativity, that doesn't feel aesthetic and illuminated, and inspired. There are forces inherent in existence that fuel negative energy... called devils, or angry/jealous gods...they do seek to mess up stuff that can be good... watch the hallmarks!.... remember there are good ones too who brought you together with guidance...and keep reminding both of love.

4th is to consciously put love acknowledgements in, constantly... admirations, compliments, wit and humor, smiles, vibes of appreciation, recognition, and heartfeltness.

5th is to vow to try not to react anymore... but to just wait a second, to remember the love foundation you agreed upon....act like your talking to a lover with sincerity.... not a separate person who's expendable. ...So apologize, accept apology, recant, and get back to harmony as fast as possible.

6th is to look at yourselves, in unity existentially...soulmates... which is merely intelligence agents in agreement....why not imagine a unity in place... pending unification....why not try to find the joy in each moment together, and plan on that continuing for a long time past this life....all one needs is just a someone... not another fish in the sea... love the one your with, because there isn't a better person... unless your facing irreconcilable differences... you can find a way, a perspective to have appreciation and gratitude... It's all about dedicating to the "Spirit of Love"... gratefully and dedicated...whoever your with... it's about finding the light in each person!

7th is to commit ... Internally... unity in mind always.... even if differences present themselves... there are only solutions, not problems! Externally, with clear signs that you'll are being more conscientious, and lovingly... and a certainty that you will make it to joy and harmony, with a solid love for others as much as the self... and a sacrifice for love at any drop of the dime... always!:)

...And in regards to friends of unfortunate circumstances...fights... the forgive is the most mature, and noble thing one can do... Everyone falls into perspectives of disdain, or distrust...Grudges, and negativity...It's not about forgetting the wrongdoing, like it never happened...that memory cannot ever be removed...it's simply about letting go of negative energy issues...and trusting that it all gets worked out on the other side....and that everything finds it's reasons for being, beyond what we would expect... and that those reasons can't be found out till the two face each other, with a neutral and open stage, and the truth pours out each others eyes ... revealing an inseparable unity....Forever!
...when we see that we are not going to escape each action and thought ever...as they are a part of a permanent database...We will naturally start to do onto others as we wish back...exclusively!....As there is no time for unresolving debates....Heavy reverse psychology games...All the negativity from the fault finders, the grudge holders, and the unyielding....Will be seen as embarrassing upon finally joining the unity in place....and seeing exactly how one wouldn't want to be treated... in reverse.

Epilogue:

Basically our spirit guide would want us to share...
So, I made a theoretical, how to meet and greet...(if there were
such a thing as a spirit guide)...this is an account of my experience, my struggles, and my insight to finding this truth...and how
it turned into finding other truths...the light, the source, the DNA,...
the counter guide...the whole gang!...I don't try to represent
them... I'm merely trying to relay a solid belief in em'...and an
inspirational reminder as well.

We are all guides to the people who ask for it...it's merely
a helping out where needed...And we all know intuitively, that it's
needed....In times of toughness, times of confusion...we know
through basic faith in life, that all things have their reasons, and
once we see and share them, It allows another after us, to avoid
the same pitfall...and that, those reasons, may just come to realization, with a little help from logic.

Angels and/or Spirit Guides are very dear to my beliefs...
though un-provable...many love the comfort that the concept
brings....it gives hope for our deceased loved ones to still be
around, to some capacity...and it gives a sense of protection,
guidance, validation, and strength....knowing we got an older soul,
who knows what it's like to be human....and knows what its like
on the other side....and what's required to get there....It's a positive imagination exercise, so as long as one understands about
the concept of no parenting....stuff happens... free will, and our
neutral set and setting take center stage.....we learn from hard-
ship... and most enjoy believing in reuniting with the deceased....
so it's what I do... I make pet concepts about god, spirits, and
reality into imaginary super fantastic things right behind our awareness... how hard is that to believe? ...to some ... impossible.... to
others... a piece of cake.......Does it matter either way?...nope!
...The reveal occurs at death... or else we just go poof... like the
ant you stepped on earlier...or is it finally in ant heaven?..
Maybe it is...I don't care...I just ponder the yonder... and get
further into it every time I try...so I keep on trying...it's working for
me...and I enjoy the challenge to recognizing such abstract concepts....and besides, the idea of me and a spirit guide, in check...
.... Is just cool!

I have done my best to relay the concepts as close to how I truly believe they are... But I don't know any more than anyone else, really... I merely have a very strong belief in a potential to realize many unrecognizable presences. These "presences"... God, Mother Nature, The Light, Old Souls... Have whispered their here! ... through books, music, passing reflections on events, thoughts, and through friends!

This is all leading to a final realization...The legendary I AM. Though we already know this... To what extent, is the question. The term enlightenment is so vague and seems to hint to a special favor from god... I hoped to squelch that misinterpretation... To one of a perpetual, and intimate revealing occurring in everyone, every second... all one has to do, is see the motion of time, see the ceasing, impermanence there in...combined with all the intelligence that goes in to maintaining a human body...Something's not staying around very long, yet seems to have a permanence of existence... Sounds like all the workings of a god sized conspiracy!

A good one, mind you... One designed, to unfold at our own pace... when we feel like it... next year... never...It doesn't matter... that's yet another clear sign of that love from above... The stuff we forget to be grateful for... forget to hold dear... Sometimes can't even remember ever having it!

But we push on... learn... and grow! We will always be *with* the now, and *in* the now,... with the one who is sourcing it... the one who illuminates it... the one who maintains health for it... and the one who guides it.

Once we get over the fears of old souls with superior awareness, aware of us... ones of positivity and of negativity... and realize there is nothing to fear... It's as it's always been... Only now, we have the power to spot negativity, as of negativity... and leave it there!... And let the positivity of the illuminated state of being... Become the standard operating procedure!

Because it's always near, no matter where, or what we're going through... we are not alone!...Or cut off from Divinity at all!... It's Just doin' what it always has, for everyone... Waiting patiently to be at your service! ...

For consultation.... as this is merely the begining of a long relationship... with our memories, our connections with other souls, and the well established old souls of the higher planes.

Terms to look up in a dictionary:

The key to most of my meaning network, synapse learning processes, and the easiest source book to assimilate the truths of the many meanings of life!

Transcendental, Light, D.N.A., Guide, Source, Time, Spirit, Soul, Separate, Aware, Recognize, Spontaneous, Empathy, Love, Totality, Monad, Compassion, Movement, Sparkle, Alone, Angel, Negativity, Realization, Cognition, Idea, Thought, Mind, Brain, Psyche, Subconscious, Selfish, Service, Demon, Bastard, Unconscious, Individuality, Ego, Liberation, Sacred, Flight, Free, Become, One, Within, Infinite, Finite, Limitless, Extraordinary, Supernatural, Metaphysical, Etheric, Transparent, Awakening, Formed, Illumination, Ecstatic, Wonderful, Amazing, Grace, Intelligence, Conspiracy, Fantastic, Perspective, Insight, Enlightenment, Emancipation, Joy, Existential, Entity, Existence, Energy, Vital, Life, Force, Flow, Harmoniously, Eternal, Simultaneously, Unity, Visions, Ancient, Mystical, Beyond, Friend, Forever, Learn, Magic, Sight, Eye, Earth, Transformation, Forever, Permanent, Mature, Graduate, Intrepid, Faith, Worry, Anger, Frustration, Understanding, Depression, Apathy, Lessons, Genius, Access, Prepare, Meditate, Acknowledge, Know, Genuine, Sincere, Moment, Meaning, Pride, Dignity, Unlearn, Remove, Notions, Limitations, Inhibitions, Invalidation, Forgive, Essence, Esoteric, Symbolic, Conceptual, Reality, Clear, Principle, Epiphany, Kind, Revelation, Heaven, Nirvana, Stoic, Attitude, Need, Truth, Potential, Preservation, Vessel, Unit.

Thank You!

In Continuum:

... I would like to spotlight the most important points covered...

A mantra of empathy for everything... makes one's light turned on permanently!

Seeing the symbolism in symbols... they tell you messages... of the truth... if one takes the clues of little symbols in everyone, every moment, and everything... and reflect on what the symbol is a symbol of.. what it might possibly be saying... The key to perceptiveness, is learning to listen deeper.

Spontaneity is a confidence in self, reality, and others... it knows it can always find a way to work out... if one puts faith into the positive expectation of stuff spontaneously working..rather than worry about things not working out, trying to control, or giving up... one can then believe in the self without focusing on the self!

The scheme of things, and the flow of day will tell one if their needing to slow down, to sharpen up, to think more, or to do it less... we are constantly consulted on how to balance with the whole of reality, life, and the beyond... Meditation puts one in sync with soul, guide, and source!

Self Righteousness is a fine line, like a tight rope to walk... to be too much is arrogant... to be too little is self degrading... we find, we come to terms with what we conceive our status in the pecking order of society to be... but in truth... no one's separate... were all in this together... and it's not forever!... so embrace time... as one can never step in the same river twice...but it's a permanent memory... and we are being watched by the unfathomed knowledgeable, and incredibly old souls.

Those who can laugh at themselves, will always be happy!

Everyday we write the book... choose your own adventure!.. trust your perceptions.. trust in your guide... guide yourself.

Drop old self concept and replace it with one of being at one, and very happy to be working for the divine, in the now... for the whole of mind, the collective of all mind, for the spiritual unity connecting us all... truly illuminated... As you are the symbol of them... a smiling saint of service to others... a hero class citizen... and a certain graduate!

Looking for joy... in the outside world is fun, and rewarding... But in light of the potential whispered to be hiding within each of us... It's like waiting for the sun to rise, while in a deep cave... it won't happen, as the only light in sight, is sight itself!

Wise unfoldment of consciousness... we participate in it... the never-ending flow of truth, reality, and mind can flux, and go in many directions... steer the vision.. stay the course.. and change it, at the same time... But be sure to listen to time as an unfoldment... a revealing of certain truths through logical mental sequencing.. Direct awareness to love, and compassion, and the unfoldment will follow accordingly...

Love imagined me... I am a thought of god... the gift of time... unwrapping itself... A thanks is all that's required for proper acknowledgement!

Don't forget about the most powerful thing one can do to regroup spiritually... just close yer eyes!... 7 seconds.. and one big breath! Refreshed, and updated as to how transcendent to the now we really are!

An important thing to do when alone... realize your not! Ancient divine surrounding within, and around... Just act like you with someone really respectable, mature, and wise... like yoda!

Just remember.. the calm air is a symbol of the presence of god.

Being a vessel to the divine... one has to remove notions of alone and separate completely... as the only thing remaining, is God... And once there is none but the one... The one vessel of love and divine wisdom... their go to guy/gal... their representative of infinite empathy... their earth angel... their friend... and initiate.

120